UNDERSTANDING SCHOOL BULLYING:
A GUIDE FOR PARENTS AND TEACHERS

Mona O'Moore

Understanding School Bullying

A Guide for Parents and Teachers

VERITAS

Published 2010 by Veritas Publications
7–8 Lower Abbey Street, Dublin 1
Ireland

publications@veritas.ie
www.veritas.ie

ISBN 978-1-84730-218-2

10 9 8 7 6 5 4 3 2 1

A catalogue record for this book is available
from the British Library.

Cover designed by Norma Prause-Brewer
Typesetting by Barbara Croatto
Printed in Ireland by Hudson Killeen, Dublin

Veritas books are printed on paper made from the wood pulp of
managed forests. For every tree felled, at least one tree is planted,
thereby renewing natural resources.

To my family
and to the memory of my parents,
Astrid and Thorleif Dahl,
and to my eldest brother, Thor.

ACKNOWLEDGEMENTS

I would like to take this opportunity to thank all the school principals, teachers, parents and students who have contributed to my understanding of bullying by their participation in the research conducted by the Anti-Bullying Centre (ABC), Trinity College Dublin. I am also indebted to those who have shared their stories of bullying with me and greatly regret not always having found the time to reply to the many touching written accounts. Without their contributions, this book would not have been possible. I would also like to pay tribute to my family for their patience and forbearance when my mind was elsewhere, but no further than trying to advance the cause of bullying prevention. Finally, I would like to express my thanks to my colleagues for their good cheer and support, especially to Lian McGuire and Murray Smith, who have been the backbone of ABC since its inception.

CONTENTS

INTRODUCTION

'Being bullied is something that stays with you for life.'[1]

At this very moment, somewhere in Ireland, there are children and teenagers who have finished a day of school that should have been about learning, personal growth, friendship and security. But this will not have been everyone's experience. For some it will have been another sad and lonely day where their sense of well-being, confidence and trust was further eroded. For others, today may have brought a new and entirely unwelcome experience: the first day that they have tasted victimisation. Perhaps this first day of bullying may bring many months or years ahead of fear, loneliness and despair, forever changing their perception of school.

Every child has the fundamental right to feel safe in school and be spared the oppression and repeated, intentional humiliation caused by bullying. Optimal learning will be achieved only when children feel safe. Unfortunately, this viewpoint is all too often ignored, as can be illustrated by a father's e-mail to me concerning his fifteen-year-old son. He wrote: 'My son, Chris, is intelligent, quick-witted and is fun and interesting to be around. He has always been liked and admired by his teachers, but despite this, Chris has been constantly bullied since his first day at school.' He further wrote that things came to a head and that Chris could no longer face his tormentors. When I arranged to meet Chris he had already lost a whole year of school due to the physical and psychological ill-effects of bullying.

School bullying is not a new problem, but it is, thankfully, receiving greater attention now than in years past. Why so? One reason is that the pervasiveness and the insidious nature of bullying is increasingly being documented and reported on worldwide. While the extent of the problem within and between countries is debated, there are few who dispute its widespread nature and the damage it may cause.

Evidence is also mounting to show that children and adolescents who are bullied or who bully others, and indeed those who have remained silent witnesses to bullying, can suffer serious social, emotional and physical ill effects. The ill effects – whether they be increased anxiety, diminished self-confidence or self-worth, fear of failure, self-harm, depression and attempts at suicide – may not only be short term or long term, but even lifelong. Bullying does not need to be endured for long before serious consequences set in. One mother, exasperated with the deterioration of her son's well-being, told me, 'In the space of a month, the effect on my previously outgoing and happy-go-lucky son has been devastating'.

There is no doubt that being subjected to bullying can hold children and adolescents back from achieving their potential not only scholastically, but also in other extra-curricular activities, such as sports. Their confidence and self-esteem suffer. Many underachieve in school as their distress conflicts with their concentration and causes them to lose the capacity to learn. Others drop out of school in order to escape the continuing torment and embarrassment of being bullied. Indeed, there are many adults today who feel that they would have been happier, more successful and fulfilled had they been spared the wilful and systematic abuse hurled at them in a persistent and seemingly relentless way. This can be illustrated by a former victim who wrote the following to me:

> I am a sixty-two-year-old woman and my life is wrecked because of bullying in school. In my case it was mental, all of it by girls starting in National School and continuing in the few years that I spent in secondary school. I had such a low self-esteem; if my mother, Lord be good to her, had time she would have noticed the huge change in me. I became more moody, crying a lot. I tried and thought about suicide definitely. Then when I got a bit older, by that I mean fifteen and a half, I really hadn't a clue and took comfort in men. I never thought I was used by men until now. But I sure was. All I say is keep advising parents that it ruins lives. I got married and lost my husband twenty-three years ago. I went back to school a few years

ago and got distinctions in all my subjects. It really still hurts that I was so stupid. I can't underestimate how my whole life was ruined. I left out depression – how could I not have that on top of the list?

If we accept Maslow's theory, as formulated in his book *Motivation and Personality*,[2] that our needs are arranged in a hierarchy – starting with our *physiological needs* (food, water, sleep and warmth), followed in turn by *safety needs* (security and freedom from threats), *belongingness and love needs* (affiliation), *esteem needs* (achievement, recognition) and, finally, *self-actualisation* (developing potential talents or capabilities) – and that the higher needs (growth needs) can only emerge as the lower ones (the deficiency needs) are fulfilled, then it is predictable that bullied children will switch their attention and efforts from learning to keeping safe. It is only when pupils feel loved, accepted and admired that they are likely to be interested in learning. A sense of security and freedom from threat also brings with it the courage to seek new experiences providing the person with further opportunities for growth and fulfilment.

The findings of the World Health Organisation[3] have greatly helped to raise the profile of school bullying. Most importantly they have highlighted the need to urgently address the issue of school bullying. In their investigation of thirty-five countries, they found that only 35 per cent of all young people in the age group of eleven to fifteen were not involved in any fighting, bullying or victimisation. Their report further highlighted that peer aggression and victimisation is a significant obstacle to healthy educational, social and emotional adjustment, and that without intervention, the young people involved 'are likely to be trapped in a snowballing pattern of negative interaction with family, teachers, peers and romantic partners'.

With bullying being so prevalent and so damaging to the well-being of the school population, not to mention the eventual negative consequences to society, it begs the question why policymakers worldwide are not investing more effort into tackling the problem, particularly as the WHO World Report on Violence and Health (2002)[4] emphasised that 'upstream investments bring downstream results'.

We know what it takes to curb bullying and this book will explore such strategies. Some countries have shown some return for their efforts by promoting an anti-bullying environment in their schools on a national scale. While Ireland does not as yet have a national policy, schools can nonetheless make a difference in the prevention of bullying. The essential ingredient is to create awareness among their communities that everyone, both student and adult, has a part to play in preventing, reducing and dealing with bullying behaviour. By doing this with conviction, schools can prevent the many associated emotions of anxiety, fear, guilt, anti-social aggression, bitterness and hatred from taking their toll on the school communities and blighting the lives of all those involved in bullying, either as victims, bullies or passive spectators.

No longer can a case be made to deny the seriousness of bullying or to justify bullying behaviour by clinging to the many misconceptions that have persisted throughout generations. This view is echoed by a former adult victim who, on hearing me talk on bullying, wrote to me about her experience and that of her school-going children. She stated how both she and her children had been bullied and harassed both in and out of school by a neighbour and her children who attended the same school. In the absence of effective intervention by the school and the then Government Department of Education, new schools had to be found for the targeted children. In her own words, the mother wrote: 'I only wish that I could have saved my children suffering from the start, but with people turning a blind eye it was totally an uphill battle. We, as parents, and our children have learnt a lot, but with this knowledge came pain and I honestly feel that my children could have done without this so early in their lives.' She went on to say: 'I have since read a lot on the subject of bullying and am wiser now. I know that inactivity to do something about and deal with bullying breeds bigger and scarier types of bullies.' Her letter very correctly concluded: 'We all need more sincerity and honesty, and also a touch of caring for another would go a long way to sort out the misery and blackness caused by bullying.'

It may well be that we may never see an end to bullying behaviour, as occasions will undoubtedly arise when people will stop at nothing to achieve their selfish goals. However, what we can ensure is that every effort is made to challenge the hurtful behaviour in such a way that allows the perpetrators to learn more socially acceptable and beneficial ways of engaging effectively with their peers and elders as they progress through life. To refrain from any form of intervention, on the other hand, sends out a very strong message of tacit acceptance of the negative behaviours. As Francoise Alsaker,[5] a well-known researcher of bullying in kindergarten, has stated, 'Children do not need to be "mean" to bully peers. They just need to learn that their behaviour is rewarding and they will keep on with their attacks.'

It is the aim of this book to provide an understanding of bullying and how to best counteract it. Throughout the book you will find statements from children and adolescents. These statements have been chosen to illustrate my viewpoints and the majority of them, unless otherwise specified, will have their source in studies that I have conducted over the years about life in school.

It is hoped that the book will go some way to motivate each reader to see the difference that they can make in preventing and reducing the level of bullying either in their homes, in school or in wider society. In making the effort you will contribute to taking the fear out of schools and in its place help to create happy and healthy children who will benefit more fully from their education.

No time should be lost in taking action to address bullying behaviour. This will be made a lot easier when we become familiar with and remind ourselves daily of Article 19 of the United Nations Convention on the Rights of the Child (1989):

> Parties shall take all appropriate legislative, administrative, social and educational measures to protect the child from all forms of physical or mental violence, injury or abuse, neglect or negligent treatment, maltreatment or exploitation, including sexual abuse, while in the care of parent(s), legal guardian(s) or any other person who has the care of the child.

Notes

1. Dubin, N., *Asperger Syndrome and Bullying, Strategies and Solutions*, London: Jessica Kingsley Publishers, 2007.

2. Maslow, A.H., *Motivation and Personality*, 3rd Edition, New York: Harper Row, 1987.

3. World Health Organisation, 'Young People's Health in Context: Health Behaviour in School-aged Children (HBSC) Study, Intermediate Report from 2001/2002 Survey' in *Health Policy for Children and Adolescents*, 4 (2004).

4. World Health Organisation, *World Report on Violence and Health*, Geneva: World Health Organisation, 2002.

5. Alsaker, F., 'Bernese Programme Against Victimisation in Kindergarten and Elementary School' in Smith, P., Kepler, B. and Rigby, K. (eds.), *Bullying in Schools: How Successful Can Interventions Be?*, Cambridge: Cambridge University Press, 2004.

HOW TO USE THIS BOOK

This book is made up of three parts. Part One consists of five chapters that aim to provide an up-to-date and in-depth understanding of bullying in a clear and concise manner. Chapter 1 looks at how we define bullying and the different forms that it takes, including cyber-bullying. Understanding what is meant by bullying is critical to finding solutions to deal with it effectively. Chapter 2 examines the many mistaken beliefs or myths around bullying. Understanding and acting on these will remove one of the major stumbling blocks to there being a greater family, school and societal commitment to countering bullying in all its shapes and forms. Chapter 3 looks at why or how children and teenagers become victims of bullying. If we can understand the cause, we can more easily prevent victimisation. Similarly, Chapter 4 examines what causes children to bully. Becoming aware of what motivates bullying behaviour will allow for the correct preventative measures to be introduced. Chapter 5 focuses on the consequences of bullying on victims, bullies and bystanders. Recognising the potential harmful effects of bullying is vital for action to be taken at a primary, secondary and tertiary level.

Part Two (Chapters 6–12) aims to provide schools and their teaching staff with a step-by-step approach for developing and implementing the critical elements of a whole school community approach to bullying prevention. Chapter 6 explains what is meant by this whole school approach, while attention is also given to the crucial steps that schools must take to develop a successful anti-bullying policy. Chapter 7 deals specifically with the role that individual teachers can play in preventing bullying. Because of the important role that self-esteem plays in the prevention of victimisation and bullying, Chapter 8 focuses on how teachers can enhance their students' self-esteem. Effective discipline is critical in reducing the level of bullying and for this reason Chapter 9 is devoted to promoting 'assertive discipline' as an effective model. Chapter 10 advises teachers how to deal with specific cases of bullying behaviour and includes guidelines on talking to parents of children involved in bullying, either as victims or bullies. As restorative rather than punitive approaches to bullying are increasingly being found to be more effective with perpetrators, Chapter 11 presents the restorative approaches, which can be easily applied by teachers in dealing with problems of bullying. Finally, to provide children with the necessary skills to resolve their own conflict and that of their fellow students, Chapter 12 is devoted to peer support strategies.

Part Three (Chapters 13–15) aims to capture the most important strategies that will help parents, in particular, to prevent and deal effectively with victimisation and bullying. Accepting that prevention is better than cure, Chapter 13 focuses on how parents can prevent their children from becoming involved in bullying, either as a victim, bully or bully-victim. Chapter 14 explains the steps that parents can take if they suspect that their child or teenager is being bullied. Advice is given in relation to each of the most common forms of bullying. Recommendations also include how parents can best approach and work collaboratively with schools when they have concerns about their child or teen being involved in bullying. In addition, there is a focus on how parents can help their child or teen overcome the damage caused by victimisation. In view of the poor prognosis for children who bully, Chapter 15 focuses on the steps parents can take if they suspect that their child is bullying others. There is a particular emphasis on developing social skills, moral reasoning and anger management.

It should also be noted that, as with my earlier writings, I frequently make reference to children and teens who are involved in bullying as 'victims', 'bullies' and 'bully-victims'. Using these terms as nouns is out of convenience only. In conversation, I endeavour to refrain from using the words 'bully' or 'victim' as nouns, favouring instead to use them only as verbs (for example, children/teens who are bullied or children/teens who bully). This is to discourage the common practice of labelling children, because it can so easily become a self-fulfilling prophecy. Also, it implies that there is no scope for change, whereas we now know that, with effective correction, victimisation and bullying can cease.

All chapters carry references or recommended reading and resources to facilitate further reading.

PART ONE

SCHOOL BULLYING: DEFINITIONS AND THE FORMS IT TAKES

School 'bullying' is an aggressive and destructive form of behaviour, which many children and adolescents use to manage their relationships while at school. This behaviour is used by such people to manipulate relationships so that they can meet their psychological needs, which may be to control, to dominate, to gain attention, to show off, to look cool or to gain status among their friends and those around them.

A good understanding of such bullying makes dealing with it a lot easier. While there is no universal or agreed definition of school 'bullying', it is generally agreed that it is a form of aggression that is intentional and unprovoked as well as being repeated over time. Some form of imbalance of power, whether physical or psychological, between the aggressor(s) and the victim(s) tends also to be involved. I will now examine each of these criteria in turn. I will then look at the forms such bullying has been found to take, both general and particular, and the factors that contribute to it.

What is 'Bullying'?
Repeated and Wilful Aggression
The repeated aggression that characterises bullying can be verbal, psychological, physical or sexual in nature, conducted by an individual or a group against others. It is not about high-spirited verbal (for example, banter) and physical games (for example, horseplay), but tends to involve very wilful and conscious acts of aggression, manipulation or both. This is in order to cause the targeted young person as much upset and hurt as possible.

The definition of the then Irish Department of Education and Science (now known as the Department of Education and Skills) in its *Guidelines on Countering Bullying Behaviour in Primary and Post-Primary Schools*[1] states:

> Bullying is repeated aggression, verbal, psychological or physical, conducted by an individual or group against others. Isolated incidents of aggressive behaviour, which should not be condoned, can scarcely be described as bullying. However, when behaviour is systematic and ongoing it is bullying.

While we may accept this definition, we need to be mindful that there are also many instances where once-off or isolated acts of aggressive behaviour can cause children and adolescents to feel harassed on a continual basis. A 'once-off' threat, for example, can cause young people to live daily in fear of that threat being carried out on them or on their friends or families. A ten-year-old, for example, having admitted to being bullied 'once or twice' in a nationwide study we carried out on school students in the school year 1993–1994, added the following: 'I was told not to tell anyone because he threatened to kill me (to stab me).' Another boy in the same class also wrote, 'I was threatened with a knife by a boy in my class.'

In defining bullying, I suggest that we have the option of including individual acts of aggression as bullying, inspired by a ringleader and cleverly perpetrated as once-off acts by different members of a group. Not including such conditions into a definition of bullying means that appropriate action may not be taken against the offending children. Worse still is that schools may not be held accountable. If this is not done, future predators or ringleaders simply need to make sure that they themselves avoid recrimination by never repeatedly acting aggressively towards their target, but rather inspire their 'henchmen' to each carry out an individual act of aggression on the targeted child. I heard from a teacher once about how a ringleader had done just that. He had passed notes to his mates on their way into school with instructions as to what they were individually expected to do to the victim on any one day, examples being 'piss on his forehead', 'stamp on his feet', etc. The victim's parents had made repeated visits to the school to impress upon the teacher that their child was having nightmares and was refusing to go to school, with the result that the parents had to drag him into school. The class teacher was initially unable to find any evidence of bullying. However, she persisted as the parents were so adamant that the cause of the boy's suffering was school related. Determined to get to the bottom of it, she eventually uncovered what was happening.

It is in relation to such cases that I believe the standard definition of bullying may fail a child. For these reasons I believe that it is timely that the definition, which has guided our common understanding of bullying – which we largely owe to Dan Olweus, the founding father of research into bullying behaviour in schools – should be revised to encapsulate isolated acts of anti-social aggression that are unjustified and serve to intimidate a child on an ongoing basis. In addition, the definition should allow for the possibility that repeated attacks of aggression on any one child should qualify as bullying, even if those attacks are not carried out by the same person, but by different individuals who together conspire to hurt the targeted child.

In advocating for a new definition to better encapsulate what is meant by bullying, consideration should also be given to whether reference should be made to the ill-effects of bullying.

As a member of the working party that drew up the previously mentioned 1993 *Guidelines*, I remember arguing strongly for leaving out any mention of the ill-effects of bullying. My concern at the time was that if the ill-effects formed part of the criteria of bullying, there was a danger that the negative behaviours that constitute bullying may not be considered unacceptable or unlawful unless there is evidence of the adverse effects. I believe it is important that bullying is judged as unacceptable and independent of its effects, in the same way that racism and sexism and other acts of discrimination are not tolerated. Victims should not have to be on the slippery slope of physical or mental ill health before they can report that they are being bullied. If we are serious about preventing bullying, it is preferable to have people come forward as soon as they recognise that they are targeted so that the unacceptable behaviours that constitute bullying can be stopped before psychological or physical damage sets in and takes its toll. This view is generally accepted with regard to other behaviours that we wish to prevent or extinguish.

We need look no further than to Ireland's drink-driving campaign to see the benefits of targeting inappropriate behaviours before such behaviours can cause harm. Increasingly, sanctions are being applied to individuals who are found to be in breach of the regulations, irrespective of whether they have been involved in an accident as a result of the offending behaviour.

In view of some of the contentious issues surrounding a definition of bullying, great care is needed when drawing one up so that maximum meaning can be provided, while potential misunderstandings can be avoided. There is no doubt that the definition in the 1993 *Guidelines* has served us reasonably well for many years. However, in view of what has been learnt about bullying since it was drawn up, there is scope for revision. This should assist schools to take more frequent and definitive actions to counter bullying, as well as help the courts to interpret bullying more accurately.

Whether or not we accept single incidents of aggressive behaviour as 'bullying', we should be aware that very young children do not place the same emphasis as older children on the repeated nature of aggressive acts.[2] Their understanding of bullying is very much based on whether the perpetrator's actions hurt them. They are, therefore, more likely than older children and adults to report once-off aggressive incidents as bullying. It is my view that their complaints should still be treated in a sympathetic manner and in a way that does not make the young child feel foolish in coming forward to tell of their own experience of 'bullying' or that of others. Rebutting children's attempts to tell is one of the biggest hurdles we face in counteracting bullying, with silence becoming the bully's best friend.

Abuse of Power

Abuse of power is also strongly associated with bullying. The imbalance of power may be rooted in age or physical and mental strength or in social groups (for example, gangs). Family background can also be a source of the imbalance of power. Certain children are made virtually defenceless by peers who threaten to have their older brothers, sisters, parents, cousins, uncles and aunts set upon them. The impact is particularly harrowing when the family is known to have a criminal background. I have direct knowledge of parents of victims who were frightened into submission after attempting to confront the tormentors. In one instance, the bully's family had a criminal record and the victim's father was warned not to involve the school authorities to put a stop to the bullying.

While the imbalance of power is often the difference in physical, intellectual, emotional or social status, it is also often the case that the victim is simply outnumbered by having to face more than one person. It is not unusual for a victim to have to try to challenge not only the ringleader, but also those who join in the bullying, commonly referred to as the 'hangers on' or 'henchmen'.

We should also be particularly mindful of the fact that a child can instantly create an imbalance of power by threatening the target with a weapon. It is to be expected that any display or threat to use a weapon is enough to place any child on their guard and to intensify the sense of fear and insecurity that surrounds being bullied.

Given that a power imbalance is at the heart of much bullying behaviour, I believe that we must also take into consideration that there will be children who have the ability to defend themselves, but who decide not to retaliate because they do not want to run the risk of being judged the aggressor by a passing teacher or told on by a vengeful 'bully' and punished as a result. There are numerous cases of children who have struck back at the bully and as a result have found themselves at the receiving end of some school punishment, such as detention or, indeed, suspension and expulsion.

However, in using imbalance of power to define bullying, I believe there is a danger that we may overlook opportunities for early intervention. I believe if we challenged all individual anti-social and aggressive acts, irrespective of any power imbalance, we would be able to interrupt the process of bullying in much the same way as is best practice in medicine. In fighting disease, prevention is of paramount importance. Failing that, the emphasis is on early intervention.

We must remember that any child, who for whatever reason is unable to defend himself or herself, when subjected to unprovoked, repeated attacks of an aggressive or abusive nature is placed in an extremely insecure and frightening position. It means that bullied children can never relax. They must always be on the lookout for the next unexpected attack. It is little wonder that their concentration is affected and their interest in learning takes second place.

The burden of victimisation is made even more intolerable by the fact that, for most victims of bullying, 'telling', referred to often as 'ratting', 'snitching' or 'grassing', is not an option. The reasons for not telling will be addressed later on. It is when children do not get the necessary help from their parents or guardians, their teachers or their peers, that they can so easily become anxious, depressed and suicidal.

As bullying is predominantly a secretive activity, carried out away from the gaze of authority, children who are bullied in school are often also subjected to appalling antisocial aggressive acts on the way to and from school – behaviours the bulliers know they would never get away with in school. One boy that I know was forcefully held back by his peers on repeated occasions from catching his bus home, a bus that his attackers knew ran very infrequently, thus leaving the child to arrive home very late. The boy would attempt to find plausible excuses for the lateness in order to avoid admitting to his parents that he was being bullied.

While it may be too ambitious to expect that a consensus will ever be reached in respect of a definition of school bullying and violence within in any one country, let alone globally, what is most important is that a definition has the capacity to help the relevant people to better understand the phenomenon. This should allow for more meaningful data to be collected and assist the development and monitoring of effective prevention and intervention strategies.

The Forms Bullying Can Take
General
In studies that I have conducted about life in school in Ireland, the pupils' responses about bullying indicate that it comes in many guises and can be direct and indirect. The faces and forms of bullying can be both mind-blowing and unthinkable and, to quote Kaj Björkqvist, an international authority on the subject of human aggression, 'inconceivable within the realm of animal aggression'.[3]

Direct Bullying

The most common forms of direct bullying that children and adolescents engage in are verbal attacks, physical aggression or assaults, gestures, extortion and cyber-bullying. Each of these overt forms of bullying will be described in greater detail further on in the chapter. However, it is important to note that children and teenagers may experience a combination of bullying behaviours.

Indirect Bullying

Indirect bullying tends to be more covert and anonymous so that the aggressor is not readily identified by the victim. Forms of indirect bullying are the circulation of nasty notes, the writing of offensive graffiti on blackboards, lockers, toilet doors or in other public places in or out of school and the damage of personal property. Defacing or writing nasty things on school books is another favourite form of indirect bullying. Cyber-bullying can also be a form of indirect and covert bullying. Because of the more concealed and secretive nature of indirect bullying, it may take longer to uncover who the offender(s) might be than it would with direct bullying.

Relational and Social Bullying

Relational bullying, while it can also be indirect in nature, causes or threatens to cause damage to peer relationships, especially to friendship and peer acceptance. Perpetrators who use this form of bullying tend to manipulate the social connections or relationships of their targets by ignoring, excluding, isolating, passing notes or spreading false information and malicious rumours about them. The motivation for these behaviours is to damage their victim's reputation and ultimately create peer rejection.

Girls are more likely than boys to engage in relational aggression. Common statements would be: 'I used to be best friends with a girl. We don't talk any more. She has a new friend. She told her new friend that I called her a slut' or, 'I am bullied by various girls who are jealous of me. They have verbally abused me in a bitchy way. I have also been physically attacked'.

In Ireland, one-quarter of girls in primary schools and almost one in three girls in post-primary schools reported that they spread malicious rumours as a way to get at their peers. In comparison, one in five boys at both primary and post-primary schools engaged in malicious rumours.[4]

Some researchers distinguish relational aggression from social aggression. Those who do tend to view relational aggression as behaviour that is intended to predominantly harm a person's friendship or feeling of belonging to a particular peer group. Specific behaviours may include:

- Withdrawing one's friendship out of jealousy or anger
- Isolating a member from a peer group
- Spreading rumours about someone to cause rejection.

The authors[5] of *Understanding Girl Bullying* are of the opinion that girls often use relational bullying 'to punish a girl or adolescent female for a perceived friendship "violation" that calls into question her loyalty to a friend'. There is no doubt that the most minor slights can so often be perceived as disloyalty and is enough to cause relational aggression. For example, for a girl to be seen talking to a friend's boyfriend or to be simply friendly to someone outside of one's circle of friends may trigger vengefulness. To be the favoured can also have similar consequences, as the following account from a third-year girl illustrates: 'I won't say her name but it all happened one night because of a boy that liked me and she got mad because I would go out with him when she liked him.'

To be snubbed or frozen out by one's friends can be very painful, causing great stress and despair, especially if the reason for the punishment is not readily understood. An example of this is a first-year pupil who stated: 'It is a boy who I thought was my friend, but behind my back or in front of me he would insult me and make me feel hurt and angry. This makes me cry.'

Social aggression, while almost indistinguishable from relational aggression, can be said to arise not so much out of conflict between two friends but out of a desire to tarnish someone's social standing or sexual reputation. The rationale for destroying reputations can be envy, jealousy and competition for social power. It can also be simply a way to beat boredom by having some fun and entertainment. The following are some examples of social bullying:

- Spreading malicious rumours and lies
- 'Cold shouldering' and isolation
- Embarrassing graffiti and the passing around of notes
- Cyber-bullying or e-bullying (electronic bullying).

Particular Forms of Bullying

In examining school bullying I have concluded that, as well as being able to break it down into three general forms, it can be further broken down into some particular forms: verbal, physical, gesture, exclusion, extortion and cyber-bullying.

Verbal Bullying

Verbal bullying is by far the most common form of bullying among both boys and girls. By verbal bullying I mean name-calling, slagging, jeering, taunting and teasing. In Ireland, in the nationwide study we carried out in 1993–1994, over 6 per cent of pupils in primary schools and 62 per cent in post-primary schools reported having experienced this form of bullying.

Is Teasing Bullying?

There are disagreements over whether teasing should count as a form of bullying. There is no doubt, however, that teasing can be a precursor to bullying. Therefore, if it is perceived to be mean, hurtful and damaging rather than playful, then in my opinion it should be described as a form of bullying. As one fifth-class girl said in our nationwide study, 'People tease me about my size. I don't think it is very funny'. I believe most people can tell the difference between teasing that is antisocial and has a malicious, demeaning or humiliating intent, and teasing that is done in a friendly spirit to enhance communication and where there is shared enjoyment. However, for fear of misinterpretation, children would do well to learn to err on the side of caution and not to tease anyone unless they are very sure of their friendship or of the sense of humour of their intended target. If a child defends his or her teasing with 'it was only a joke', or 'I was only messing', it suggests that the teasing was at best a controversial target and at worst hurtful and indicative of bullying.

It should be noted that words can be of a highly personal nature, with verbal attacks being directed not only at the child or adolescent in question, but also at their friends and families. Name-calling and slagging can carry messages that are highly emotionally charged, such as getting at the person's physical appearance, for example, 'big ears', 'carrot top', 'cabbage head', 'pudding face' and 'fatty', and also their personal hygiene, for example, 'smelly' – names which can stick for a lifetime. A fifth-class boy commented, for example, 'It's horrible – I keep being bullied and they keep calling me rubber lips. I hate them.'

A documentary, *Bully For You*, by Eamonn Devlin[6] illustrates just how an abusive verbal label can stick and the potential it has to destroy the victim's sense of well-being and to haunt the victim indefinitely into adulthood. Eamonn Devlin courageously told his own story and that of others who had been devastated by the bullying they experienced while at school. Those who felt able to speak as adults were all scarred emotionally from this experience.

Clothes that children wear can also be a source of considerable verbal bullying, as can academic success or failure. I know of one boy who deliberately started to fail his maths tests to be spared from the daily verbal attacks of his jealous tormentors. By failing a few tests in succession he was finally spared.

Being verbally smart can often stop verbal 'slagging', as the last thing a 'bully' wants is to look foolish for want of a smart response. It is easy to see, therefore, how children with general or specific learning difficulties, who may lack the necessary verbal skills and quick wit, are at particular risk of repeated verbal assaults.

Verbal Attacks on the Grounds of Discrimination

The abuse so characteristic of verbal bullying can also be very discriminatory, getting at, for example, a person's sexual orientation, religion, ethnicity or nationality. Typical comments would be: 'I am bullied because my father is Chinese'; 'We get called chinks, blackies, etc.'; 'I am called horrible names about my father's nationality. I get called a "nigger"'. Children who are German or who have German parents tend also to be targeted with, 'I am called a "nazi" because my mother is German'. A study[7] funded by the Irish Youth Foundation found, for example, that post-primary, school-age lesbian, gay, bisexual or transgendered people in Ireland are at particular risk of name-calling, teasing and bullying in their everyday lives. Half of all these students admitted to being bullied. Over 71 per cent of them reported that they were called nasty names and that they were teased about their sexuality and made fun of (37 per cent occasionally, 9 per cent once a month, 25 per cent once a day). A presentation to the Oireachtas Education Committee by the BeLonG To youth service highlighted the difficulties that gay pupils face as a result of bullying.[8]

Increasingly, electronic devices such as mobile phones and computers are used to carry abusive and destructive verbal messages. Over 24 per cent of gay students reported that they had been bullied in this way. This form of bullying, now commonly referred to as cyber-bullying or e-bullying (electronic bullying), will be explored later in this chapter.

We found that boys are more inclined than girls to verbally abuse their fellow pupils on the grounds of diversity, for example, colour and race.[9] Insulting and humiliating someone on the basis of their sexuality, nationality and religion and other diversities undoubtedly reflects prejudice, ignorance or both. The increased prevalence of this form of abuse reflects the growth over the past fifteen years of different nationalities and cultures in Ireland. With this in mind, we should strive even harder to tackle bullying in our schools.

Physical Aggression

Direct physical aggression includes all forms of pushing, shoving, poking, grabbing, hair-pulling, hitting, spitting, biting, scratching, punching, head-butting, tripping someone up and endless other forms of physical attacks. Examples of physical aggression that children subject each other to inside and outside of school are as follows:

> 'People walked on my head and spat on me' (fourth-class boy).
>
> 'One girl called me names about my teeth. If I say something back to her she kicks me and hits me across the head' (fifth-class girl).
>
> 'Sometimes they kick me in my leg and punch me in the face' (fourth-class boy).
>
> 'When I was alone outside the library two girls pulled my hair and hit me in the face' (second-year girl).

Physical bullying can also take the form of more serious physical assaults, which require medical intervention, for example, kicks to the groin, the breaking of fingers, arms and legs or injuries to the head. Such bullying is more commonly associated with boys. In Ireland, we found that over one in three of both primary and post-primary school boys engage in some form of physical aggression.

There is evidence, however, that girls may be currently exhibiting more physical aggression than they did in the past. In primary schools the level of physical bullying reported among girls has risen from 15 to 19 per cent and in post-primary schools it has increased from 11 to 14 per cent. What is certain is that both boys and girls of primary school age in Ireland regard physical bullying as the worst sort of bullying.[10] Physical bullying is often written off as 'horseplay', 'only messing', 'pretending' or 'just a game' when challenged. While children and teenagers do play roughly, care needs to be taken with such 'games', as they can so easily lead to more vicious and repeated attacks. Just how vicious physical bullying can become and what girls are capable of, especially when there is no early intervention, can be illustrated by the following report:[11]

> The six-strong pack of teenage pupils were caught on camera taunting terrified Nadia Dorrington, 14, before viciously punching and kicking her to the ground. They are then seen pulling out her hair in clumps while other pupils stand around shouting vile abuse. The attack starts off with one girl in uniform beating the victim before her friends join in. Distraught Nadia was left with cuts and bruises to her face and bald patches on her head from where clumps of her hair had been pulled out in the shocking assault. To humiliate her even further, the footage was uploaded to the video-sharing internet website YouTube under the title 'Fighting a Dirty B****'. It has been seen by hundreds of people including the girl's devastated family.

It was reassuring to learn from the report that Nadia's parents immediately complained to YouTube with the result that the video was removed. We also learnt from the report that Nadia had suffered bullying at her all-girls' school for three years, but that the school 'failed to act saying they had no proof'.

The silver lining in respect of this ugly event is that the parents gained evidence of the incident and as a result were able to bring their complaints to both the school and the police. The parents of Leanne Wolfe,[12] who took her life and had experienced years of bullying by other teenagers in her local community, were not so fortunate. Only after her death did they gain evidence of a vicious campaign of bullying against her, where many forms of bullying had been used, from cyber threats to direct and indirect physical aggression.

A very worrying present trend is the fight clubs that are increasingly taking place. This is where students, boys in particular, arrange fights, often outside of the school, between rival gangs. The fights are filmed and posted on YouTube to embarrass the loser and increase the status of the winner. These fight clubs can sadly be used to force a victim into fighting against his or her will.

Physical aggression that is indirect can also involve the interference with or damage to a child's or teenager's personal belongings. This is very vividly illustrated in a DVD on bullying called *Silent Witnesses*.[13]

Gesture Bullying

This form of bullying can be very intimidating and frightening. It consists of many different forms of non-verbal aggressive and threatening gestures, which can convey very intimidating and frightening messages. Very common is the 'dirty look', the cold stare or the 'look' that can kill. Also popular is the gesture of slitting the throat. Other horrifying acts, which pupils know are a reality, that can so easily be gestured are, for example, 'bog washing' or 'being urinated on', not to mention 'pointing the gun' and 'pulling the trigger'.

A physical or intellectual difference that may exist can also be intentionally gestured in order to humiliate or ridicule the disliked person. Thus, rather than calling someone, for example, a 'cripple', a 'faggot' or a 'retard' to their face, gesturing it can have an equal impact.

Exclusion Bullying

Exclusion bullying, which, as we have seen, is particularly prevalent among girls, is particularly hurtful because it isolates the child from his or her peer group. It can be very difficult to combat such bullying as it directly impacts on the isolated pupil's self-confidence and self-esteem. The experience may be all the more painful if the reason for exclusion is not known and when there are a significant number of friends involved in the exclusion bullying.

For a child or adolescent to assist in excluding a friend who has given them no personal grief or reason to be vengeful reflects a level of social insecurity and strong dependency on group membership. Such children clearly perceive rejecting a friend as a means of securing their position within the group, thereby avoiding, as much as possible, a similar fate to that of their friend. It is perhaps not surprising that it is the children with the greatest sense of self-worth who can more easily resist peer pressure and take a defending role in a bullying situation.

In our nationwide study of 1993–1994, we found 20 per cent of girls versus 8 per cent of boys in primary school and 14 per cent of girls versus 5 per cent of boys in post-primary school used 'cold shouldering' and exclusion as a means of bullying their peers. In our more recent study, however, the gap between boys and girls appears to have narrowed, but the level of indirect aggression has increased. We noted, for example, that 34 per cent of girls and 26.4 per cent of boys at primary school and 29 per cent of girls and 18 per cent of boys at post-primary school reported having been left out, excluded or ignored. This may reflect that young people are more willing than before to report being involved in aggressive behaviours or that they are instead reverting to forms of aggression that are less easy to detect or prove.

A most poignant account of exclusion bullying is the following, written by a boy who told of his experience in a school magazine[14] after the school had initiated awareness-raising activities on the subject of bullying:

> My first term this year was very distressing and I never seemed to fit in. It was hard, no one to talk to, no one to laugh with or play with, no one to help with troubles and, worst of all, no one who loved and cared for me. My work was declining rapidly and I could do only one thing, which was to try my best to persevere and fight the pain of things that were hurtful and not helping.

Extortion Bullying

Extortion bullying consists of demands for money, possessions or equipment. These demands may often be accompanied by threats (sometimes carried out) if the victim does not give what is demanded. Victims may also be dared or forced to either steal items for delivery to the aggressor(s) or initiate or join in in some anti-social act. These tactics often serve the purpose of incriminating the victim, while at the same time demonstrating who is 'boss'. Extorting bad behaviour, which has to be acted out in class, naturally puts the victim at risk of punishment from the teachers, as well as causing fear of reprisals if the truth were told, thus placing the victim in a no-win situation.

Cyber-Bullying

Cyber-bullying involves the use of electronic devices such as mobile phones and computers to carry abusive and destructive verbal and visual messages. The most commonly used methods are as follows:

- **Text Messaging.** If texts are of a sexually explicit nature, the process of sending them is referred to as 'sexting'.
- **Camera or Video Clips.** This involves using camera phones to send pictures, sometimes of a very sexual nature. With the help of image-editing software programmes, photos can be doctored so that the victim is depicted in a compromising, embarrassing or sexual manner.
- **Internet Postings.** This involves using any of the social networking sites, such as Bebo, YouTube, MySpace and Facebook, to post messages or images, or to create detailed profiles which may also contain pictures.
- **E-mail.** This is one of the most popular forms of digital communication. E-mails can also contain pictures and can reach thousands of people at any one time. Although e-mails are traceable, there is no guarantee that the account holder is the person who sent the e-mail. It is also possible to sign individuals up to sites or lists without their knowledge. This can cause a host of unwelcome e-mails.
- **Mobile Phone Call.** This is a popular means to communicate verbally but, as with standard telephones, can be a source of silent

calls. Mobile phone numbers can be blocked to hide the identity of the caller.

- **Online Chat Rooms.** Chat rooms provide an opportunity for people young and old to meet and discuss a topic online. There is even scope to pick an avatar or a symbol (for example, a character or an animal) to represent themselves and through whom they communicate. People can adopt identities that are very different to their real life identity, for example, their gender, their age and their nationality. The purpose may be liberating, but it may also be done with the intent of tormenting or insulting other members.
- **Instant Messaging.** This involves real-time communication via the internet with friends who are on a contact list. There is scope to send inflammatory messages and abusive and compromising images, and also to pretend that they come from someone else on the list.
- **Websites.** Normally a website is developed to promote a business or to provide information on topics of interest. However, websites can also be developed with the sole purpose of denigrating and humiliating a person. This is done by providing very personal information and by altering photographs so as to portray the person in a very compromising or sexual manner. Web pages can also be used to set up internet polls so that votes can be cast with regard to any personal attribute, from the most to the least attractive girl in the school.

Data collected for the World Health Organisation's 'Health Behaviour in School-aged Children' study showed that, in Ireland, 44 per cent of eleven-year-olds, 59 per cent of thirteen-year-olds and 65 per cent of fifteen-year-olds use electronic media communication five days or more a week. Contrary to popular belief, the study also found that the more children and teenagers use electronic media communication, the more friends they have and the more time they spend face to face with their friends in the afternoon and evening. Mobile phones have, of course, made arranging to meet so much easier, as it overcomes the need as before to make fixed appointments in school. We can now all be on the move and still be reached.

However, in recognising that cyber-communication has the potential to promote and strengthen friendships, it also has to be acknowledged that it has the potential to cause serious damage to those at the receiving end of what may be abusive, belittling, embarrassing and humiliating messages and images. Messages can also be extremely frightening, as was experienced, for example, recently by a very brave teenager, who came forward on RTÉ's nine o'clock news[15] to say that after school she would receive threatening text messages, such as, 'Watch your back, I'm going to kill you'.

There is a popular belief that online threats simply reflect teenagers having fun, but according to two researchers in the USA,[16] a considerable proportion of threats made online are actually carried out in school, highlighting the relevance of cyber-bullying in the real world.

The fact that cyber-bullying may penetrate any space in which victims find themselves makes it very different from more traditional bullying. The victim essentially has no escape. Not even their homes can afford them proper protection, unless, of course, they switch off all electronic communication devices once in the door. Even switching off does not in reality offer respite, as they may be worried about what might be said about them. In contrast to the more traditional 'bully', the 'cyber-bully' is also able to conduct his or her bullying campaign anonymously without ever having to face the victim, leaving the victim with the added distress of not knowing the identity of the aggressor.

The knowledge that abusive or threatening messages can reach a much wider (and potentially global) audience than is possible with the more conventional forms of bullying is in itself immensely disconcerting, frightening and demoralising. Not knowing who the perpetrator(s) are naturally affords victims with far fewer opportunities to both name and shame their aggressor(s) and defend themselves. This in itself has the potential of increasing the power of the perpetrator, who can damage the victim by any or all of the following cyber behaviours:

- **Rumour Spreading.** With mobile phones and computers, messages can be sent very quickly and can reach an unlimited number of people.
- **Flaming or Trolling.** This involves sending insulting messages intended to inflame emotions of others so that a flame war is created in 'public' places, such as in a chat room, on a social

networking site or within interactive virtual world environments (for example, Second Life).

- **Impersonation.** This involves the perpetrator using the victim's password to send or post insulting and hurtful messages to selected people pretending they are coming from the victim. The cyber-perpetrator can also alter the victim's profile by adding and disclosing details that are either very personal to the victim and his/her family or simply untrue. To create maximum upset the perpetrator can then alert the world, so to speak, to the updated profile, which can then spark off endless responses.

- **Outing and Trickery.** This is when a victim has shared confidences with someone who then forwards it on to others. A victim can also be tricked into confiding in a classmate who then shares the information with others.

- **Online Exclusion.** This can be achieved by knocking a victim off an e-mail or buddy list so that he/she is kept in the dark as to what their circle of friends may be up to.

- **Physical Threats.** This involves online threats to a victim's physical safety and well-being.

- **'Happy Slapping'.** This is the term used when direct physical assaults are filmed using a camera phone. The image(s) are then forwarded on to classmates by means of mobile phones and e-mail, or posts on the web (for example, YouTube) for anyone to see in order to cause the victim maximum hurt and embarrassment. What might appear hilarious at the time can sadly end in tragedy. Triston Christmas, an eighteen-year-old in the UK, was hit so hard that he fell backwards, hitting his head off a concrete floor. While he lay on the ground bleeding, his attackers proceeded to photograph him. They then went on to a party and posted the images of Triston online. Triston died a week later. Other 'Happy Slapping' incidents have led to suicide, the embarrassment being too great to bear for the victim.[17]

Factors that Contribute to Various Forms of Bullying

I have looked at the forms bullying can take, both general and particular. In contributing to these forms, I have concluded that there are two main factors at work: gender and age.

Gender

There are considerable differences in the forms of bullying behaviour displayed by boys and girls. Generally speaking, while boys and girls rely most heavily on verbal bullying, boys tend to use physical forms of aggression more than girls do.

Ireland's first nationwide study, which I conducted over fifteen years ago, showed that 32 per cent of primary and 35 per cent of post-primary boys were physically hurt, compared to 15 per cent of primary and 11 per cent of post-primary girls.[18] These marked differences have also been found in a more recent national study conducted ten years later by Stephen James Minton and myself.[19] While the level of physical aggression was almost identical for the boys in the intervening years, there were indications that girls were becoming more physically aggressive. We found that now over 19 per cent of girls at primary and over 14 per cent at post-primary school reported that they were physically hurt. The increase in physical aggression among girls is evident in many cultures, especially in Ireland, according to the most recent WHO report.[20] It most probably reflects the decline in gender differentiation. Instrumental also will be the media's increasing portrayal of women as aggressive and ambitious and at times even resorting to physical aggression to achieve their aims.

Valerie Besag, author of *Girls' Friendships, Fights and Feuds,* points out that it is more usual for girls to attack those familiar to them, whereas boys are more likely to attack a stranger. She compares the phenomenon to the pub brawl, which so often stems 'from a challenge directed at a stranger, whereas women are more inclined to choose their target for gossip and ostracism from those among their acquaintances'.[21] She also makes reference to the tendency of girls when challenged about their bullying behaviour to readily offer a rationale and justification for their attacks, although their excuses are rarely based on fact.

Age

The age of the child can also determine the form that the bullying takes, although differences tend not to be found until children are around eight years of age. Young children whose verbal skills are not yet so well developed tend to use physical aggression to get at someone. However, girls tend to become less physically aggressive with age.

Boys, on the other hand, steadfastly hold on to physical aggression. Nevertheless, as boys grow older they do also revert to more verbal aggression, and as verbal ability increases with age so does the sophistication with which both boys and girls can target someone with words. Indirect bullying also becomes more popular as children develop social skills, which enable them to be scheming, manipulative and clever enough to avoid detection.

I am very much of the opinion that everyone who engages in an aggressive act will tend to weigh up the likely effect that an aggressive act may have on the victim against the likely danger involved in getting caught in the act. This view has been referred to as an effect/danger ratio or a cost/benefit ratio. What becomes clear is that the tormentor assesses the relation between the effect of the intended strategy and the danger involved in him/her being hurt physically, psychologically (becoming embarrassed, ridiculed or ashamed) or socially (the loss of friendships). It is reasonable to expect that the aggressor will try as much as possible to maximise the impact on the target, while at the same time minimise the risk to him or herself. It is important to the aggressor, therefore, to find a strategy that can serve both purposes, i.e. be effective in attacking the target while avoiding detection. Taking this view, it is not difficult to see why children and teenagers, as they gain in social and cognitive skills, choose means other than direct physical aggression to get at their victims. It can also explain why direct verbal acts are preferable to direct physical acts, the former being much more difficult to prove because there may be no visible injuries and, as is often the case, it becomes 'one man's word against the other'. It also explains why indirect and cyber acts of aggression gain in popularity as children develop the necessary verbal and social skills. Also, the fear of being identified and counter-attacked makes indirect bullying most attractive. It is also tempting to attribute the greater use of cyber-bullying acts by girls in post-primary schools in Ireland to this effect/danger ratio.

In the next part of this book we will look at the options that are open to dealing with bullying in its different forms.

Key Messages
- Bullying can be both direct and indirect.
- Bullying can include:
  - Verbal bullying (about race, gender, sexual orientation, religion or disability)
  - Physical bullying
  - Gesture bullying
  - Exclusion bullying
  - Extortion bullying
  - Cyber-bullying:
    - Girls have a higher incidence of being cyber-bullied
    - Boys have a slightly higher incidence of being the cyber-bully
    - Victims reported phone calls and text messaging as the most common forms of cyber-bullying
    - Cyber-bullies, especially boys, favour taking camera and video clips as a means of cyber-bullying
    - Ideas for intervention can best be gained from the pupils themselves.
- Bullying can focus on *any* form of difference.
- Bullying is rarely a single incident.
- Bullying tends to be an accumulation of many small incidents, each of which when taken in isolation and out of context may seem trivial.
- Bullying is when someone is singled out and robbed of his or her dignity day after day, week after week, month after month and, in some cases, year after year.

Notes

1. Department of Education and Science, *Guidelines on Countering Bullying Behaviour in Primary and Post-Primary Schools*, Dublin: The Stationery Office, 1993.
2. Guerin, S. and Hennessy, E., 'Pupils' Definitions of Bullying' in *European Journal of Psychology of Education*, 17 (2002), pp. 249–261.
3. Björkqvist, K., 'Sex Differences in Physical, Verbal, and Indirect Aggression: A Review of Recent Research' in *Sex Roles*, 30 (1994), pp. 177–188.
4. O'Moore, A.M., Kirkham, C. and Smith, M., 'Bullying Behaviour in Irish Schools: A Nationwide Study' in *Irish Journal of Psychology*, 18 (1997), pp. 141–169.
5. Field, J.E., Kolbert, J.B., Crothers, L.M. and Hughes, T.L., *Understanding Girl Bullying and What to Do About It: Strategies to Help Heal the Divide*, Thousand Oaks, CA: Corwin, 2009.
6. Devlin, E., *Bully For You*, Triplevision Productions Ltd., broadcast on BBC (NI), September 2008.

7. Minton, S.J., Dahl, T., O'Moore, A.M. and Tuck, D., 'An Exploratory Survey of the Experiences of Homophobic Bullying Amongst Lesbian, Gay, Bisexual and Transgendered Young People in Ireland' in *Irish Education Studies*, 27 (2008), p. 2.

8. Kelly, O., 'Most Gay Pupils Bullied in School-Youth Service', *Irish Times*, 3 July 2009.

9. Minton, S.J., 'Students' Experiences of Aggressive Behaviour and Bully-Victim Problems in Irish Schools' in *Irish Educational Studies*, 29 (2010), pp. 131–152.

10. O'Moore, A.M. and Minton, S.J., 'The Hidden Voice of Bullying' in Shevlin, M. and Rose, R. (eds), *Encouraging Voices*, Dublin: National Disability Authority, 2003.

11. *The Sun*, 1 May 2009.

12. Jennifer Hough, 'If Someone Had Reached Out, It Could Have Made a Difference', *Irish Examiner*, 20 October 2008.

13. *Silent Witnesses*, a DVD and workbook to assist schools and parents to prevent bullying. Produced by Animo Communications, 2006.

14. *Our Times*, Wesley College, December 1994.

15. RTÉ, nine o'clock news, 17 June 2009.

16. Hinduja, S. and Patchin, J.W., *Bullying Beyond the Schoolyard: Preventing and Responding to Cyberbullying*, California: Corwin Press, 2009.

17. Kowalski, R.M., Limber, S.P. and Agatston, P.W., *Cyberbullying: Bullying in the Digital Age*, USA: Blackwell Publishing, 2008.

18. O'Moore, Kirkham and Smith (1997), op. cit.

19. Minton (2010), op. cit.

20. McInerney, S., 'Ireland Hit by Rise in Teen Girl Bullies', *Sunday Times*, 26 July 2009.

21. Besag, V.E., *Understanding Girls' Friendships, Fights and Feuds: A Practical Approach to Girls' Bullying*, London: Open University Press, 2006.

2 BULLYING: THE MISTAKEN BELIEFS AND THE WARNING SIGNS

There are many mistaken beliefs or myths around bullying and these pose a challenge to the development of a greater family, school and societal commitment to countering bullying in all its shapes and forms.

The extent to which adults and, indeed, children intervene in cases of bullying so often belies their knowledge, values and attitudes towards bullying. It is only to be expected that teachers, parents and young people will have different views and levels of knowledge about bullying behaviour, which will undoubtedly determine their concern and guide their actions when confronted with bullying.

Over ten years ago, I reported that a significant proportion of teachers in our primary schools and post-primary schools did not feel that bullying was a problem in their schools. This may explain why so few teachers were reported by their students to intervene in cases of bullying.

Hopefully, with the increased awareness that has taken place in schools and workplaces in the intervening years, this situation has improved. However, in spite of the increasing recognition that bullying, harassment and ridicule has been linked to several incidents of school shootings in the US and Europe, many children are still growing up in homes and attending schools where they hear adults profess to the fact that bullying reflects normative behaviour. Children may grow up hearing adults comment as follows:

'There is no bullying in our school.'
'Bullying is a normal part of growing up.'
'I was bullied at school and it didn't do me any harm.'
'Bullying is character-building, it toughens you up.'
'It will make a man of him.'

'There was bullying at school but it didn't hurt anyone.'
'Bullied children need to learn to deal with bullying on their own.'
'Sticks and stones can break your bones but names can never hurt you.'
'Don't tell or you are a grass.'

It is to be expected that attitudes such as those expressed above might be a reflection of people who have either not suffered bullying or been witness to someone who has had the grim experience of being singled out and picked on in a deliberate, systematic and hurtful manner. On the other hand, supporting attitudes of bullying may reflect a lack of emotional empathy or an inability to identify with the pain of victimisation. There may also be adults who are in denial of the ill effects, preferring to take the easy way out by turning a blind eye to bullying behaviour.

It would, of course, not be altogether unreasonable to speculate also that the myths are perpetrated from one generation to the next by adults who in their own childhood have bullied others and who are still lacking the necessary understanding, compassion, shame or empathy to see the downside to bullying. This is not to overlook the fact that defensive views regarding bullying may well also be held by individuals who do not wish to admit to having themselves been bullied for fear of being judged as weak, therefore buying into the misconception that victims are inadequate and unpopular.

There will also be adults who see the positives in bullying, having perhaps themselves bullied others or seen others bully in order to realise their occupational ambitions. I remember a father exclaim rather indignantly after a talk that I gave to parents on the subject of bullying that 'surely if dog eats dog in the adult world, children should be allowed to do the same while at school so as to prepare them for the adult world'. When adults share such sentiments it is clear how necessary education is around the subject of bullying. On the other hand, there are adults who require no further education beyond that of having themselves had the experience of being bullied in the workplace. On meeting with them, they would confess readily to having been party to the mistaken belief that the fault somehow lies with the victim. However, their own experience of bullying told them that no amount of past achievements or coping skills made them immune or saved them from being singled out by work colleagues or superiors who were in pursuit of their own naked ambitions, or those of their organisation.

Just as any adult can become a victim so also can any child or teenager. It is vital, therefore, that we all join in with the Department of Education and Skills in recognising, as they do in their *Guidelines to Countering Bullying in Primary and Post-Primary Schools*, that any pupil can be a victim or perpetrator of bullying behaviour.

If we were to take each myth as listed above, and they are by no means exhaustive, we would find that each one is flawed. Not one school that took part in our two nationwide studies reported that they were free of bullying. From the first study I estimated that there were at least 20,000 primary pupils and 7,400 post-primary pupils in Ireland who were subjected to frequent bullying – that amounts to once a week or more often.[1] Ten years later we found[2] that the situation had worsened with even more children and teens at primary and post-primary schools reporting frequent bullying. While no school was immune to bullying, it has to be said that it was more common in those schools where little was done to prevent it.

There is no doubt that some adult myths have probably come about and are bandied around in the mistaken belief that it may be comforting to the victim to know that it is a normal part of growing up and, in addition, that 'it is good for you'. However, the reality is that it only serves to undermine the victim further. By normalising bullying or expecting the victim to retaliate causes the victim to feel anything but normal. Indeed, self-blame and feelings of inferiority tend to result. Victims are also at risk of getting seriously hurt or fatally wounded if the aggressor is bigger or stronger or has the backing of a larger group.

Telling is a Weakness

In addressing bullying, the reluctance to tell ('don't rat') presents as one of the greatest challenges for educators. The many reasons why children, whether as victims or onlookers, find it difficult to tell are as follows:

- Fear of reprisals
- Shame, humiliation, degradation
- An inability to perceive how to go about changing the situation due to low self-esteem and feelings of helplessness
- An unwillingness to publicise their unpopularity
- An inability to explain due to emotional or intellectual constraints – maybe too confused, upset or afraid
- An inability to perceive actions such as teasing, social exclusion, etc., as bullying
- Seeking help confirms the taunts of being incompetent, being a baby or being stupid, and they fear losing respect of teachers/parents by their inability to cope
- The bully may claim that it is only a game, meaning the victim might be seen as a liar or being over-sensitive
- Victims may feel this is the way they should be treated, especially if they have low self-esteem
- No confidence in an adult's ability to help.

The responses of parents and teachers to children's attempts at telling of their own or that of their friend's experience of being picked on are critical in shaping children's attitudes to telling. One primary fifth-class pupil illustrated this through the following account: 'I am being bullied a lot. I cannot do anything, they are too big. I cry. My mum says I should not tell. I am very sad.'

For children to hear that 'telling' is a sign of weakness and, therefore, something to be ashamed of is naturally going to influence their attitude to reporting bullying, whether as a victim or a witness. My husband, for example, was reared on the following saying:

> Tell tale tit,
> Your tongue shall be slit,
> And all the doggies in the town,
> Will have a little bit.

No child should be dismissed in their efforts to tell. It must be remembered that children who can fight their own battles tend not to seek help. Thus, those who tell are generally those who feel they cannot effectively defend themselves. But all too often their accounts are not taken seriously, with the result that they come away feeling humiliated, ashamed and no closer to knowing how to stop the bullying.

No child should be left to feel guilty because they do not have the necessary skills to put a stop to bullying. Neither should children have to feel that they must tolerate the dread and fear of school owing to the insults, humiliation, threats, exclusion or physical injury that is so much part of bullying.

It is understandable why those with a propensity to bully may be keen to reinforce the taboo on telling, as it gives them the perfect weapon to silence their victims, as well as those who may witness the abusive behaviour. Evidence of this in an extreme form can be found from accounts in our national newspapers of killings that have resulted from individuals intentionally or unintentionally exposing criminal activity. For example, the *Irish Times*[3] reported: 'Garda believe that the father of two was targeted because a member of his family gave evidence against a leading member of the McCarthy-Dundon criminal gang in a criminal trial four years ago.' It is understandable how accounts such as these will send shock waves through society about the wisdom of telling. However, Mr Steve Collins, the father of Ray, who was fatally shot, did society an immense service when he courageously told Miriam Callaghan on *Prime Time*[4] that he would act as a witness in the future if called upon to do so. In other words, Mr Collins recognises, as did our famous Irish philosopher and statesman, Edmund Burke, that 'the only thing necessary for the triumph of evil is for good men to do nothing'.

It is clearly of benefit to all in society, therefore, if the reluctance to 'snitch' is put to bed. Instead, children should be reared and educated to appreciate that to seek help for oneself or for others by telling is to behave responsibly. Not to do so is to condone the wrongdoing or to act irresponsibly.

If children grow up with the right values and receive the correct education about telling, they will soon learn to distinguish between good and bad 'telling'. Most importantly, by encouraging children to tell of wrongdoing, no opportunities will be lost for corrective action to be taken and it will also enable practical help to be given to the

49

victims. All too often children are told to stand up for themselves, but they are rarely told or shown how best to do this. Specific strategies, such as assertive behaviour, should be discussed and demonstrated, something which I will discuss later (see Chapter 13).

How Common is Non-Reporting of Bullying?

The reluctance to tell is universal, and other countries are experiencing the same problem, but in Ireland it appears to be particularly bad. We found that nearly half of primary pupils and two-thirds of post-primary pupils had not told anyone at home that they were being bullied. The situation was even worse with regard to telling teachers. There were two-thirds of primary pupils and the vast majority of post-primary pupils who had not let their teachers know that they were being bullied. However, some comfort can be gained from the fact that those who were frequently bullied were somewhat more inclined to tell.

The reluctance of pupils to reveal to anyone at home or a school staff member that they are being bullied increases steadily as they advance through primary and post-primary school (see Appendix). Buried among these statistics are accounts such as this from a fourth-class primary school pupil: 'My skirt was being pulled up and I didn't like it. I was pushed by a girl and broke my leg. I didn't say anything to my teacher.'

The finding that so many children and teens are unable to talk to their teachers about their victimisation reflects the extraordinary strength of the taboo regarding telling. It also reflects a fear of not being believed and a fear of reprisals. For example, one mother seeking help for her son wrote the following:

> My son who loved school for two years suddenly began to hate it and pleaded with me to let him stay at home. This went on for a while until eventually he woke up at night and I held him, and he began to tell me, when he was half asleep, 'They are at me'. 'Who?' I said, and he mentioned two names. When I followed it up the day after, he told me not to do anything as they would kill him. He really believed it.

Gender Differences in Reporting

We found in our nationwide study that boys of all ages found it more difficult to tell parents of their victimisation than girls. The difference between boys and girls was most marked at post-primary school. The reasons for the gender differences are not clear. It is possible that the age-old view holds true, namely that boys find it more difficult than girls to talk about their emotions and that the older they get, the harder it becomes as they are ever more expected to conform to the male stereotype of being macho and able to sort out their own differences. Interestingly, however, we found that boys at primary level were more likely to tell their teachers than were girls. Might it be that girls at this age find it is more difficult to convey that they have been bullied than boys because of the more social and relational nature of the bullying to which they are subjected? Quite apart from the fact that physical bullying may be easier to describe and, indeed, to resolve, it may also be more believable from a teacher's perspective, especially because there may be some visible proof of an injury.

Self-Esteem and Reporting

It should be noted that it is the victims with higher self-esteem who find it easiest to tell. Perhaps their greater confidence and feelings of self-worth makes them feel less ashamed about telling. They may also be more able to articulate the problem or they may hold sufficient belief that those in authority will take action.

It is promising that by sixth year students see a greater virtue in telling, possibly prompted by greater confidence and maturity (see Appendix).

Reporting of Cyber-bullying

Reporting on cyber-bullying is no easier than admitting to traditional bullying. In our most recent study on cyber-bullying, we found that less than a quarter had told their parents and as few as one in fifteen had told their teachers. Boys were the most reluctant to tell anyone, including their friends.[5]

It is clear from our findings on non-reporting that every effort must be made to challenge the taboo of telling and to make it safe for children to tell an adult, either a parent or teacher, whenever they feel that their own efforts to stop the bullying are not succeeding. To prevent the shame that is associated with telling, adults must provide leadership in dispelling the misconception that the victim somehow is always at fault. In a later chapter on who bullies, it will become evident with whom the burden of guilt should lie.

To promote the reporting of bullying, adults must also become more effective in their interventions. Greater attention must be given to develop more empathic and trusting relationships between children and their teachers, because there is little doubt that many children have every reason to be afraid of telling.[6] They will have experienced or even been witness to reprisals that have resulted from clumsy interventions on the part of teachers and parents. Parents, rather unwisely, have been known to go after the perpetrator(s) themselves, with dire consequences for the victim. Teachers, also rather foolishly, have been found on occasion to announce in front of the whole class that a victim's parents have been in to lodge a complaint, causing further humiliation to the victim. In respect of cyber-bullying, care needs to be taken to not over-police it, as this acts as a strong deterrent to reporting it. It is preferable to focus on cyber-safety and help victims to develop strategies to stop the bullying.

Warning Signs of Bullying

Bearing in mind the reality that many victims and onlookers of bullying do not seek help, it is vital for parents and teachers to spot the warning signs. These are as follows:

- Unexplained bruising, cuts or damaged clothing
- Visible signs of anxiety or distress – refusal to say what is wrong
- Unexplained changes in mood or behaviour, for example, becoming increasingly withdrawn, clingy, attention-seeking, aggressive towards family members
- Out of character behaviour in class, for example, disruptive, attention-seeking (possibly due to a threat or dare)
- Deterioration in educational achievements, loss of concentration, interest and enthusiasm in school
- Erratic attendance due to reluctance to go to school
- Lingering behind in school after class

- Increased requests for money from parents or stealing money (to pay off sources of intimidation)
- Loss or damage to personal possessions or equipment
- Artwork expressing inner turmoil.

While the tell-tale signs of cyber-bullying tend to be indistinguishable from the signs of traditional bullying, there are some that are specific to cyber-bullying. These are as follows:

- Appears upset when online or coming offline
- Appears upset when viewing a text massage
- Withdraws from social interaction with peers
- Possible drop in academic performance.[7]

A significant proportion of cyber-victims also remove themselves from the online venue in which the cyber-bullying occurred, with as many as one in five feeling forced to stay offline completely for a period of time.[8]

In addition to all of the above signs and symptoms, the likelihood of there being psychosomatic symptoms, such as headaches, stomach aches and general insomnia, is also great. Bed-wetting and sleepwalking can also be indicative of the psychological stress associated with bullying. One student told me about her experience as a child. She had been admitted to hospital several times without anyone being able to diagnose the source of the severe stomach pains until, after leafing through what had become a very thick medical file, the paediatrician in charge picked up her rag doll and asked if the doll was happy. At this she broke down and all was revealed, with the result that the school finally had to take account of the bullying that had taken place over the course of many years without the knowledge of parents or school staff.

Understandably, it is not always possible, especially for teachers, to rely on tell-tale signs for the detection of bullying. Some victims are simply very good at both covering up their plight by showing no outward signs and at providing plausible excuses if questioned. There will also be instances where any signs of bullying are masked by the cunning and devious nature of the perpetrators. Whenever an adult is present or in sight, they can be quick to cover up and fake a good relationship with the victim. However, once the adults are out of sight, the hard knocks are delivered. With such guile on the part of pupils, it is perhaps not too surprising, as our nationwide study showed, that for post-primary students most bullying actually occurs in the classroom rather than outside in the corridors or playground. It also lends support to the finding that youngsters who bully, contrary to popular opinion, can be skilled manipulators, possessing good theory of mind abilities.[9] Their social skills enable them to organise their classmates effectively and target a victim while avoiding detection.

Change in Mood

Of all the signs and symptoms of being bullied, I believe the most telling one is that of a change in mood. Knowing the mood of their child best, parents or guardians are naturally in a better position than teachers to discern whether there is a significant change in behaviour. They are also in a better position to judge whether there is something at home or at school that may be causative of the change in mood and behaviour (increased irritability, tearfulness, loss of confidence, withdrawn). Parents can also more easily notice if there is a significant drop in the number of friends calling to the house or of invitations to go out after school, which in teenage years tend to increase.

It is important to be aware that bullied teenagers who would normally seek to hang out with their peer group may find it extremely difficult to meet friends after school for fear of future victimisation. One boy told me that he was even unable to go into his local town for an errand because of the fear of bumping into the boys who were tormenting him at school. To this day, as an educated young adult, he says that he still experiences residues of anxiety when he heads into town. His greatest test was when he had become a third-level student and found himself in a queue where he recognised the shop assistant to be one of the 'bullies'. His immediate reaction was to leave the queue, but with the help of considerable positive self-talk he was able to overcome his anxiety and, to his relief, go through with the purchase.

To spot victimisation in a teenager may be more difficult than in a younger child, because the tell-tale signs of victimisation can be confused with the inner turmoil or stress and strain that so often characterises adolescence.[10] For example, twelve- to fourteen-year-olds experience significantly more negative effects than ten- to twelve-year-olds, and this is generally related to negative life events connected with family as well as school and peers. As teens grow older, more is expected of them socially, emotionally and educationally, both at home and at school. The pressures to live up to these expectations can cause undue conflict, especially if pressure exceeds capability. In order to escape from the tension and the pressure of life, adolescents can so easily turn to alcohol, drugs and, indeed, anti-social behaviour.

It should be noted also that the tell-tale signs of bullying can, in addition to being symptomatic of 'adolescent turmoil', reflect other problems, such as substance abuse, teenage pregnancy, uncertainty around sexual orientation or family problems.

The symptoms may also reflect physical violence or bullying in the home by siblings or, indeed, parents. For example, in our nationwide study, approximately one in twenty students reported that they were being bullied in their homes. Some typical statements were:

> 'I am bullied by my brother and, it may sound stupid, but he always hits me and slags me. I hate it.'
> 'My parents are going to get separated. My father beat me up last Monday and yesterday my mother gave me a black eye.'
> 'I am bullied by my father. He beats me up when he comes home from the pub and takes it out on me.'

Bullying in the neighbourhood can also be a problem and should not be underestimated. Over 6 per cent of primary pupils and 10 per cent of post-primary pupils in our nationwide study gave written accounts of neighbourhood bullying. For example, one girl wrote, 'This girl goes to this school and threatens me at home with her big gang.'

Of great concern is that some of the bullying and violence that some of the pupils experience in their neighbourhood is not just conducted by their peers, but also by adults. One second-year boy, for example, had this to say: 'I got a kick in the head by a man on my road twice. He thinks he's a karate expert!' Another boy had this to say: 'I got beaten up several times by strong, bald men in their thirties. They threatened me with a bottle of Vaseline.'

Other places where bullying was reported outside of school were at sports clubs, youth clubs and at Scouts. It is not difficult when reading the accounts to sense the victims' considerable feelings of frustration, distress and, indeed, powerlessness.

With bullying being so widespread, a rule of thumb for any reader that may be faced with any out-of-character behaviour that causes concern and persists over time is to take action. To investigate any of the tell-tale signs will mean taking the initiative to talk to the child or teen. This will probably not be easy in relation to peer bullying for the reasons that I have outlined above. However, you will be surprised what a relief it will be to your child once 'the cat is finally out of the bag'. It should be stressed that even if no ready solution comes from the initial talk, it is in seeking the cause that an effective cure can be sought.

Key Messages

- The mistaken beliefs associated with bullying need to be dispelled, as they help to justify bullying behaviours and to make the victim out to be at fault.
- Bullying is not 'normal' or socially acceptable.
- 'Telling' to prevent injury or to correct inappropriate behaviours should not be condemned; the taboo of telling only serves to safeguard and protect the bully.
- Children should not have to deal with bullying on their own. Bullying can have serious repercussions for the mental and physical health, as well as career opportunities of both victims and bullies.
- Parents, teachers and others can dispel the myths by instilling the correct values and engaging in exemplary behaviour.
- A high proportion of children and adolescents do not tell adults that they are being bullied.
- The predominant reasons for not reporting bullying to parents and teachers are shame at the lack of popularity, the inability to defend oneself, fear of reprisals and inept actions of parents and teachers. There is also the dread of being condemned as a 'snitch'.

- If any of the warning signs are present and bullying is suspected, take the initiative to talk to the victim and, if necessary, seek expert advice from school staff or an outside agency.
- Try to get to the root cause of the bullying as that will speed up recovery.

Notes

1. O'Moore, M., Kirkham, C. and Smith, M., 'Bullying Behaviour in Irish Schools: A Nationwide Study' in *Irish Journal of Psychology*, 18.2 (1997).
2. Minton, S.J., 'Students' Experiences of Aggressive Behaviour and Bully-Victim Problems in Irish Schools' in *Irish Educational Studies*, 29 (2010), pp. 131–152.
3. 13 April 2009.
4. RTÉ, 14 April 2009.
5. O'Moore, M. and Minton, S.J., 'Cyber-Bullying: The Irish Experience' in Quin, C. and Tawse, S. (eds), *Handbook of Aggressive Behaviour Research*, New York: Nova Science Publishers, 2009, pp. 269–292.
6. O'Dowd, E., *An In-depth Analysis of the Lack of Reporting of Bullying by Girls*, unpublished MEd (Aggression Studies) Thesis, Trinity College Dublin, 2009.
7. Kowalski, R.M., Limber, S.P. and Agatston, P.W., *Cyberbullying: Bullying in the Digital Age*, USA: Blackwell Publishing, 2008.
8. Patchin, J.W. and Hinduja, S., 'Bullies Move Beyond the Schoolyard: A Preliminary Look at Cyber-Bullying' in *Youth Violence and Juvenile Justice*, 4 (2006), pp. 148–169.
9. Sutton, J., Smith, P.K. and Settham, J., 'Social Cognition and Bullying: Social Inadequacy or Skilled Manipulation?' in *British Journal of Developmental Psychology*, 17 (1999), pp. 435–450.
10. Murray, M. and Keane, C., *The Teenage Years*, Dublin: Mercier Press, 1997, in association with RTÉ.

3 | WHO ARE THE VICTIMS OF BULLYING?

Are Victims of Bullies Wimps or Peculiar in Some Way?

One of the many misconceptions that surround the subject of bullying is that children who are bullied are different in some way. The fact is that any student, through no fault of their own, may be bullied. This view is also strongly endorsed by the Department of Education and Skills in their *National Guidelines to Counter Bullying in Schools*. Essentially, all it may take for a child or adolescent to be bullied is to be in the wrong place at the wrong time, and to be faced with a more forceful person who has the intent to hurt and to isolate. It is not unusual, therefore, to meet victimised children and teens who are attractive, popular and academically successful, but who have no means of escaping their bullies.

I know of one school, for example, who refused to change an acknowledged perpetrator to another class giving the reason that it would unsettle him coming up to the Junior Certificate exams. Quite apart from sending out the message to the victim and his parents that the well-being and achievements of the acknowledged perpetrator were valued more than that of the victim, it also highlights just how trapped a victim can become.

Anyone who has tried to challenge children who bully will have found that they tend to justify what they are doing by emphasising that the victim is different in some way. For example, they may claim that they:

- have a different accent;
- wear different clothes;
- have a different religion;
- come from a different country;

- have a different social or economic background;
- have a learning disability;
- are gifted.

If there is no real difference, those who bully may invent one, be it that they label them, for example, 'gay', 'slut', 'retard' or 'smelly'. However, while not all children who are bullied start out being different in any significant way, it is recognised from available studies and anecdotal evidence that there are children and teens who are more likely to be targeted than others. They tend to have:

- an anxious, sensitive, shy, insecure and cautious temperament;
- fewer good friends;
- low self-esteem;
- a passive, non-aggressive or non-assertive manner;
- an emotionally reactive manner;
- clumsy entry behaviour when trying to join a peer group.

'Being different' has been studied very carefully by Helen Sweeting and Patrick West.[1] They found from a sample of eleven-year-olds that being overweight, having physical disabilities, such as visual, speech or hearing impairments, increased the likelihood that a child will 'experience the additional burden of being bullied'. Children who were physically unattractive and academically weak were also found to be more at risk of being targeted. In addition, children who suffered longstanding or (more serious) limiting illnesses were significantly more likely to express frequent teasing/bullying. These findings are supported in the recent *Growing Up in Ireland* study of nine-year-olds.[2]

Sweeting and West recognised, however, that there were a certain proportion of children in the study who had been bullied in spite of having the most desirable characteristics, such as having been rated as the most physically attractive and above average in ability. This goes to show that it is not merely 'being different' that causes a child or adolescent to be bullied, but instead it is more likely to be the way they handle being picked on.

Short stature is another physical characteristic for which there is scientific evidence to show that it increases the likelihood of pupils being bullied and to suffer social isolation.[3] However, like certain other differences, short stature tends to be age- and gender-specific. Twice as many boys of short stature were found to be bullied when short stature became noticeable in adolescence.

However, again as with some of the earlier mentioned differences, it is not inevitable that it will promote bullying. This can be illustrated very clearly by a story told to me by one of my sons. It involved two classmates of his, John and Shane (both pseudonyms). They were both thirteen-year-old boys at the time and both were below average height for their age. Shane was forever being bullied, with constant reference being made to his small stature. My son reported that on entering the classroom one day he saw that Shane was very upset and as John entered the classroom along with others he blurted out to John for all to hear, 'How come you get away with not being picked on seeing as you are as small as I am?' Hearing this, John immediately took one step forward, as if on stage, and remarked in a most assured, confident and rather cocky manner for all to hear, 'I make small look good'. It is clear to see why John was not singled out for his height, as he obviously had the capacity to ward off potential attackers with a quick wit, sharp tongue and confident manner.

The behavioural, social and physical characteristics that have been found to increase the likelihood of being bullied typically fall into two main groups, the majority of which are submissive and passive and the minority being provocative. Dan Olweus[4] was the first to document the distinction between passive and provocative victims. Essentially, the passive group is made up of children who tend to be submissive, fearful, withdrawn, anxious, cautious and prone to showing emotion when upset. They avoid confrontation and lack the confidence to get support from their peers. Passive victims, especially boys, also tend to be physically weaker than their peers. For this reason they tend to be less effective in physical activities, such as gym, games and sports. It is of note that Helen Sweeting and Patrick West, whose study I referred to earlier, found that high athletic achievement was associated with no experience of victimisation. However, this finding cannot be taken as a rule of thumb, as I have come across both children and adolescents who have shown a great aptitude for sports, but have been targeted by peers who have been jealous of their achievements. Indeed, to show that young people who are good at sports are not immune from being bullied, we chose to include in our DVD, *Silent Witnesses*,[5] a teenager who suffered victimisation because his peers were jealous of his sporting success.

Provocative/Aggressive/Bully-Victims

While victims, whether traditional or cyber, are generally characterised as being more anxious,[6] there is a sub-group of victims who are prone to provocative, aggressive and hostile behaviour. Valerie Besag,[7] one of the first authors to write about bullying, states that 'they tease and taunt yet are quick to complain if others retaliate'. Dan Olweus,[8] who was aware that they comprise only the minority of victims, found that, like their more passive counterparts, they were physically weaker than their peers. In addition, he found them to be anxious, insecure, unhappy and distressed. However, when insulted or attacked they would react in a hot-tempered manner and fight back, but not very effectively. Sometimes they would also bully those weaker than themselves, and in doing so would share characteristics of children who bully. This sub-group of victims were generally known as provocative victims, but are increasingly now referred to as 'aggressive victims' or 'bully-victims'. The terms tend to be used interchangeably.

Most recent research[9] has shown the sub-group of victims to be more proactive and impulsive than pure victims, and to be more reactively and less proactively aggressive than children who bully only. They are also more likely than pure victims to be physically bullied. When they bully they tend to use more physical than verbal forms of bullying.

Aggressive victims also have fewer friends than pure victims, and it has been observed that teachers tend to be less sympathetic towards them, thus not readily intervening, as they feel that they deserve the treatment they get from their peers. The finding that they are more socially isolated than pure victims has been taken to account for why they bully more physically than they do verbally. The view is that verbal bullying is more dependent on supportive group dynamics than physical bullying.

In our Irish nationwide study,[10] we found that 14 per cent of primary school children and 4 per cent of post-primary students were bully-victims. This showed that there were at the time as many as 1,787 children who could be classified as bully-victims (1,341 at primary school and 446 at post-primary). These children had the lowest self-esteem of all the sub-groups in the study.[11] They see themselves in comparison to pure bullies as being more troublesome, having lower intellectual and school status and being less physically attractive, more anxious, less popular and more unhappy and dissatisfied.

In an earlier study,[12] we found that the more frequently the victims bullied their peers, the more inadequate they felt about their behaviour and their intellectual and school status. The victims who frequently bullied were also the least happy and satisfied. When compared to pure victims, they were also found to be less emotionally stable, more excitable, more disregarding of rules, more astute and more tense. Judging from what we know of cyber bully-victims, they are not distinguishable from their traditional counterparts.[13]

There is some suggestion[14] that aggressive victims may come from more chaotic home backgrounds than pure victims. However, more research is needed to determine if they really do experience more coercive parenting and different forms of family conflict, which may account for their more reactive and physical style of aggression.

It is clear from the symptoms that aggressive victims portray, especially those who are frequently bullied and who also bully others frequently, that they form a distinct group.[15] It is imperative that they should receive appropriate professional support to help them overcome the behavioural and emotional difficulties that hinder their development. How this can best be achieved is something that I will address in Chapter 10.

Asperger Syndrome and Bullying

Before leaving this chapter, it should be noted that evidence is mounting to indicate that children with Asperger Syndrome may be more at risk of being bullied than any other category of children with special needs. The early study[16] of 'Bullying in Dublin Schools', for example, showed that one in six children with mild general learning difficulties in ordinary schools were bullied frequently (once a week or more often) in contrast to one in twenty students who had no learning difficulties.

However, this pales in significance when we take children with Asperger Syndrome into account. Having reviewed the available research literature and anecdotal information, Rebekah Heinrichs[17] refers to them in her book as the perfect targets, and that they are almost without exception bullied. This is because they share many of the characteristics of both passive and provocative/aggressive/bully-victims. Essentially, they 'lack the social skills and social support to counter their attackers and, therefore, often become chronic targets of bullying'. However, Rebekah Heinrichs correctly points out that 'no child has the necessary social skills to stop severe bullying without adult intervention and support'.

How Many Children are Victimised?

Based on our nationwide study of bullying in Irish primary and post-primary schools[18] and our subsequent national study,[19] we can say with confidence that there are at least one in five primary school children who can be classified as a pure victim (bullied only) and one in seven who are bully-victims (both bullied and bully others). Figures from Northern Ireland are even higher.[20]

If we look closely at nine-year-olds, we will see that little has changed to curb the level of victimisation since the *National Guidelines on Countering Bullying in Schools* were issued to schools in 1993. Back then I found that 40 per cent of nine-year-olds reported that they were bullied and the very same percentage was reported in the most recent national longitudinal study (GUI) funded by the Office of the Minister for Children.[21] In an average class size of twenty-four children, we can expect, therefore, that there will be approximately seven to eight victims of bullying. It is little wonder that the Department of Education and Skills receive an average of ten complaints from parents a week.[22]

In post-primary schools there is at least one in eight pupils who is bullied and one in twenty who both bully and are bullied. If we look to our fifteen-year-olds as we did to our nine-year-olds, we learn from our most recent figures that 43 per cent of students reported having experienced at least one form of bullying, while 14 per cent experienced three or more forms of bullying.[23] A most conservative estimate, therefore, for an average class of twenty post-primary pupils would be that at least three to four students are bullied, either as a pure victim or bully-victim.

Figures that we have for cyber-bullying show that there is an additional one in ten post-primary students who are victims of cyber-bullying and a further one in twenty-five who are both a bully and a victim. Over two-thirds of cyber-victims are traditional victims. A significant number of cyber-victims are also traditional bullies.[24]

It should be noted that more boys than girls are bullied in each year in primary and post-primary school. However, more girls than boys reported being cyber-victims. In Ireland, most bullying in primary school occurs in the playground, whereas for post-primary students it happens more often in the classrooms.

Also to be noted is that schools differ in the prevalence of victimisation and bullying. Factors such as school and class size, ability grouping, single-sex and co-education, advantaged and disadvantaged statuses, urban/rural locations and the social composition of the schools all affect the level of victimisation.[25]

Key Messages

- Any school child or adolescent through no fault of their own can be victimised.
- Peer victimisation is widespread with almost one in three primary and one in five to six students at post-primary school experiencing being bullied, either as a pure victim or a bully-victim.
- Some young people are more at risk of victimisation than others.
- Differences, for example, 'physical', 'intellectual' or 'belonging to a minority group', may prompt victimisation, but it is the attitude and behaviour in response to the negative behaviours that will determine whether the bullying persists.
- The risk factors that promote an escalation of bullying among those targeted are a passive or submissive manner and having few friends.
- A minority of young people who are bullied also bully. Because they tend to have an aggressive/provocative manner, they are referred to as 'provocative' or 'aggressive' victims or 'bully-victims'.
- Intervention and prevention programmes need to target both the submissive (pure) victims and the aggressive/provocative/bully-victims.

Notes

1. Sweeting, H., and West, P., 'Being Different: Correlates of the Experience of Teasing and Bullying at Age 11' in *Research Papers in Education*, 16 (2001), pp. 225–246.

2. Williams, J., et al., *Growing Up in Ireland National Longitudinal Study of Children: The Lives of 9-Year-Olds*, Minister for Health and Children, Dublin: The Stationery Office, 2008.

3. Voss, L.V. and Mulligan, J., 'Bullying in School: Are Short Pupils at Risk?', questionnaire study in a cohort, *British Medical Journal*, 320 (2000), pp. 612–613.

4. Olweus, D., *Bullying at School: What We Know and What We Can Do*, Oxford: Blackwell, 1993.

5. *Silent Witnesses*, a DVD and workbook to assist schools and parents in preventing bullying. Produced by Animo Communications in association with the Anti-Bullying Centre,TCD, 2006.

6. Corcoran, L., Connolly, L. and O'Moore, M., *Cyber-Bullying: A New Dimension to an Old Problem*, presented at the Psychological Society of Ireland's Annual Conference, Tullow, Co. Carlow, 20–23 November 2008.

7. Besag, V.E., *Bullies and Victims in Schools*, Milton Keynes, England: Open University Press, 1989.

8. Olweus (1993), op. cit.

9. Unnever, J.D., 'Bullies, Aggressive Victims and Victims: Are they Distinct Groups?' in *Aggressive Behaviour*, 31 (2005), pp. 153–171.

10. O'Moore, M., Kirkham, C. and Smith, M., 'Bullying Behaviour in Irish Schools: A Nationwide Study' in *Irish Journal of Psychology*, 18.2 (1997).

11. O'Moore, M. and Kirkham, C., 'The Relationship Between Bullying and Self-Esteem' in *Aggressive Behaviour*, 27 (2001), pp. 269–283.

12. O'Moore, M. and Hillery, B. (1991) and O'Moore, M. (1997) in Michelle Elliott, 1st and 2nd Edition of *Bullying: A Practical Guide to Coping for Schools*, London: Longman, in association with Kidscape.

13. O'Moore, M. and Minton, S.J., *Bullying, Cyber-Bullying, Gender and Personality*, submitted for publication.

14. Unnever (2005), op. cit.

15. Cook, C.R., Williams, K.R., Guerra, N.G., Kim, T.E. and Sadek, S., 'Predictors of Bullying and Victimisation in Childhood and Adolescence: A Meta-Analytic Investigation' in *School Psychology Quarterly*, 25 (2010), pp. 65–83.

16. O'Moore, M. and Hillery, B., 'Bullying in Dublin Schools' in *Irish Journal of Psychology*, 10 (1989), pp. 426–441.

17. Heinrichs, R., *Perfect Targets: Asperger Syndrome and Bullying – Practical Solutions for Surviving the Social World*, USA: Autism Asperger Publishing Co., 2003.

18. O'Moore, Kirkham and Smith (1997), op. cit.

19. Minton, S.J., 'Students' Experiences of Aggressive Behavior and Bully-Victim Problems in Irish Schools' in *Irish Educational Studies*, 29 (2010), pp. 131–152.

20. Collins, K., McAlveavy, G. and Adamson, G., 'Bullying in Schools, A Northern Ireland Study' in *Educational Research*, 16 (2004), p. 1.

21. Williams, J., et al. (2008), op. cit.

22. Sheehy, C., '10 Bullied Pupils Take Complaints to Top Each Week', *Evening Herald*, 29 May 2010.

23. Eivers, E., Shiel, G. and Cunningham, R., 'Ready for Tomorrow's World? The Competences of Ireland's 15-Year-Olds' in *Pisa 2006 Main Report*, Dublin: Educational Research Centre, St Patrick's College.

24. O'Moore, A.M. and Minton, S.J., 'Cyber-Bullying: The Irish Experience' in Quin, C. and Tawse, S. (eds), *Handbook of Aggressive Behavior Research*, Hauppauge, NY: Nova Science Publishers, Inc., 2009.

25. O'Moore, Kirkham and Smith (1997), op. cit.

4 WHO ARE THE CHILDREN WHO BULLY?

It is my strong belief that bullying behaviour is learned, therefore 'bullies' are not born, they are made. As all bullying is a form of aggressive behaviour, a distinctive characteristic of children who bully is their aggressive attitude towards not only their peers, but also towards adults, like their parents and teachers. Constitutional factors may play a part in aggressive behaviour, but it is recognised that factors within the home, school and wider society greatly influence the development of aggressive behaviour.

The Commission on Children and Violence, convened by the Calouste Gulbenkian Foundation, reported in 1995 that the most powerful risk factors in violent behaviour are:

- Violent and humiliating forms of discipline
- Attitudes that approve of violence in the home and the world outside, i.e.:
  - o Adults behaving violently towards each other
  - o Adults behaving violently towards children
  - o Macho role models
  - o Preferences for violent images on TV and film
  - o Racial hatred
  - o Violence in sport
- Poverty and poor living conditions.

From birth, children learn an extraordinary amount of behaviour through observation and imitation of those around them. This means that children who grow up with encouragement, praise, tolerance, fairness, respect and love will learn to be respectful, tolerant, caring and show love to others. Those who are subjected to hostility, ridicule, disrespect and cruelty risk developing not only a poor self-concept, but also risk treating others in a similar manner.

The factors that have been found specifically in the home to contribute to aggressive behaviour and bullying are:

- Lack of love and care
- Too much freedom
- Inconsistent discipline
- Permissive management of aggressive behaviour
- Violent outbursts on part of adults
- Excessive physical punishment.

Michael Rutter,[1] a most eminent child psychiatrist, together with his co-researchers, has demonstrated that schools can also make a difference to a child's level of aggression. The factors that have been found to contribute to aggression and disruptive behaviour in schools are:

- Inconsistent and inflexible rules
- Poor staff morale
- Inadequate supervision
- Punishment that is too harsh, abusive or humiliating
- Few incentives and rewards for non-aggressive behaviour
- Curriculum that affords too few feelings of success and achievement.

The ability to learn by observation and imitation has been shown by Albert Bandura, a most distinguished psychologist, to be restricted not only to face-to-face behaviour in homes, schools and neighbourhoods, but also to behaviour that is portrayed on screens. Sadly, children are only too often exposed to aggressive and violent ways of behaving on their screens through TV, cinema and video games. Studies have shown that children who constantly view violence on TV and video/DVD develop greater physiological arousal, more aggressive tendencies and less empathy with victims of aggression. In effect, exposure to an overdose of screen violence in the comfort of one's own home or cinema can lead to a serious decrease in reactivity or sensitivity to violence. Video games also have the effect of increasing aggressive thoughts, feelings and physiological arousal. Indeed, playing a realistic violent game stimulates more aggressive feelings and arousal over the course of the game than does a non-violent game.[2, 3]

A most recent study of college students of diverse ethnicity has shown that exposure to even a short period of media violence can influence attitudes towards victims of violence and the enjoyment of violent content. In effect, the process of desensitisation has the power to make real-world violence more acceptable or normative. The authors of the study make the point that a person desensitised to violence 'may not be concerned, empathetic or sympathetic toward the victims of violence and will be less likely to help the victims of violence'.[4] The danger for society is that the process of desensitisation will cause individuals to accept that violence is normative.

This view may seem far-fetched, but perhaps not so when one considers that there is a clinical technique used in behaviour therapy, which is to desensitise individuals to anxiety-arousing stimuli by exposing them repeatedly, while in a relaxed state, to the feared object. In the United States, the military are known to prepare soldiers for the battlefield by having them play violent video games in order to desensitise them to the anxiety-provoking violence that they might meet. After a diet of screen violence, it is clearly hoped that when faced with the enemy they will be in a position of déjà vu and any potential killing will become automated and, thus, not seen as such a big deal.

Some of you reading this chapter may recall an incident in Waterford where a group of young children savagely set upon a ten-year-old and beat him up badly, kicking him while on the ground until he was unconscious.[5] Worse still, they left him to suffer his injuries, probably not even knowing or caring whether he was dead or alive. It is incidents like these that one feels are fuelled by being a witness to or a victim of violence beyond the home or school. It is not unusual for films to depict victims of violence to be able to tolerate savage beatings and manage somehow to bounce back or re-emerge without ever seeming to die from their injuries. Such viewings must inevitably give children a false impression of what the body can take before it is fatally wounded.

I am aware that the relationship between screen violence and aggressive behaviour is still a controversial one. However, I have yet

69

to hear how the defenders of screen violence explain away the power of imitation, which, after all, is the key to a very successful advertising industry. In other words, how come, on the one hand, we are expected to be influenced by all the visual advertisements that appear on our TV, cinema and computer screens, yet, on the other hand, we are supposed to be resistant to imitating violent behaviour?

Characteristics of Children who Bully

Children who bully do not all share the same traits. They come, as J.S. Jackson states in her *Kid's Guide for Dealing with Bullies*, in all shapes and sizes, adding that 'you can tell bullies more by how they act than by how they look'.[6] Having said that, they do tend to have one or more of the characteristics listed below. The list is by no means exhaustive and I have deliberately left out some traits, as they tend to be controversial as well as gender- and age-specific. Their self-concept is one such trait and the jury is still very much out on this. The undisputed characteristics are as follows:

- They have a strong need to dominate socially, to feel powerful and to be in control
- They have a low level of frustration and are easily angered
- They have low self-control and are impulsive and reactive
- They are not anxious
- They do not take responsibility for their behaviour but rather blame their victim
- They have a tough poise
- They see aggression as a favourable quality
- They are oppositional, defiant and aggressive
- They are insensitive and derive pleasure in hurting others, including animals
- They lack emotional empathy
- They engage in other forms of anti-social, rule-breaking behaviour, like stealing, vandalism and substance abuse
- They are loud and attention-seeking
- They may have been bullied themselves.

Distinctions have been made between different types of bullies, for example, confident bullies, anxious bullies, passive bullies and bully-victims.[7] However, more recent research has pointed to only two distinct groups, pure bullies and bully-victims. Pure bullies bully only, whereas bully-victims both bully and are bullied. Both groups share certain characteristics that I have listed above, but there are some traits that set them apart.

The pure bullies are the most common type of bully. They tend to be fearless and domineering and show little empathy for others. They have a very positive attitude to aggression and will tend to target their victims in a predatory or a proactively aggressive manner.

Pure bullies, while they do act alone, are also known to hang out together, reinforcing each other's aggressive behaviour. The fact that they tend also to have 'hangers on' to assist or reinforce them in their aggressive acts can make victimisation an extremely frightening and humiliating experience for those targeted. Pure bullies, when challenged over their negative behaviours, have no compunction about denying it and, if anything, may try to pin the blame on the victim, implying that they were at fault in some way. Indeed, most recent research[8] has provided strong evidence that shows that post-primary students who bully are prone to show moral disengagement by rationalising and justifying harmful acts against others. They not only legitimise their aggression in order to make a harmful act less harmful and to eliminate self-censure, but they also expect positive outcomes from their negative behaviours. The authors of these studies argue that the expectancy of positive and favourable outcomes could be a tangible reward, enhancement of self-esteem or status, peer admiration, and so on.

The pure bullies of both primary and post-primary age in our large-scale Irish study[9] had a view of themselves that was only average. Their overall self-esteem was lower than that of their peers who did not bully or who were not victimised. Similar findings have now been reported for cyber-bullies.[10] Examination of the different domains of self-esteem in our Irish study indicated that their feelings regarding their behaviour, their intellectual and school status and their happiness and satisfaction were significantly more inadequate than that of their non-involved peers. The more frequently they bullied others the lower their feelings of self-esteem in respect of these domains and of their global self-esteem. Further significant differences were found in relation to anxiety. The pure bullies, although restricted to those of post-primary age, were less anxious than their peers who reported no involvement in bullying, either as victims or bullies. Those who bullied most frequently were the least anxious teens.

It is of note that the pure bullies did not differ from their non-bullying peers in respect of their physical appearance and their popularity. This result finds support in international literature. However, it should be noted that there is some evidence to suggest that as aggressive children advance through school, their popularity begins to wane. The more extreme they become in their social and physical aggression, the more their peers will reject them. This has been reflected in the self-ratings of children and teens who admit to bullying. Our study of self-esteem found, for example, that all the girls and boys who admitted to bullying their peers on a frequent basis, regardless of whether they were also victimised, viewed themselves to be more unpopular than bullies who only occasionally or moderately bullied.

The lower anxiety and positive feelings about their physical appearance and their popularity that characterised the pure bullies may help to explain why bullies are so often rated by others as confident and having relatively good self-esteem. It seems fearlessness and 'good looks' may be mistaken for good self-esteem.

Personality and family relationships have also been found to play a large role in the bullying behaviour of six- to sixteen-year-olds.[11] Pure bullies were more extroverted (outgoing), neurotic (emotionally unstable) and psychotic (tough-minded) than children not involved in bullying, either as bully or victim. Higher levels of neuroticism were found in girls who bullied than in boys. In addition, primary-aged bullies were more neurotic and psychotic than post-primary bullies. Also, those who bullied tended to have difficulty expressing their emotions freely towards the various members of their family. Indeed, the bullies exhibited an ambivalent relationship to their mothers and fathers, which was in contrast to the positive relationships shown by their counterparts who did not bully.

These findings support earlier international research, which has found that children who bully tend to come from homes where they experience:

- a lack of warmth and involvement;
- permissiveness of aggression;
- physical punishment and violent emotional outbursts;
- negativism on the part of the mother;
- negativism between the parents.

In view of the relationships found between bullying and child-rearing methods, it is reasonable to conclude that 'love and involvement from the parent(s) who rears the child, well-defined limits on which behaviours are permitted and which are not and use of non-physical methods of child-rearing create harmonious and independent children'.[12]

Bully-Victims

Insofar as we can judge from the research that is available to us, bully-victims are indistinguishable from children whom we described in Chapter 3 as 'provocative' or 'aggressive victims'. Essentially, the readiness of bully-victims to blurt out what is on their mind before thinking, due to their impulsive nature and poor self-control, means that they tend to be regarded as socially inept, provocative and confrontational. It is, therefore, not surprising that they have fewer friends than pure bullies.[13] Among them will be students with Asperger Syndrome and ADHD, as well as those 'bullies' who Olweus labelled 'passive bullies, followers, or henchmen'. He distinguished these bullies from the 'typical bully' as they tend not to take the initiative. As a group, he also found them to be 'fairly mixed and also to contain insecure and anxious students'. In our most recent study,[14] while we found them to be as tough-minded as pure bullies, they were more neurotic (emotional). The same was true for cyber bully-victims. Indeed, a most recent synthesis of a collection of studies showed bully-victims to experience the worst of both worlds. The authors[15] concluded that 'they resemble victims by being rejected and isolated by their peers and resemble bullies by being negatively influenced by their peers with whom they interact'.

There is some speculation that bully-victims have different socialisation experiences than pure bullies and pure victims. For example, it has been found that they have been more harshly treated

73

and more physically abused by their parents than have pure bullies and pure victims. Compared to the other two groups, bully-victims have also been reported to experience the least parental involvement, with there being a lack of effective communication. In addition, there is some international research which tentatively points to bully-victims coming from a more chaotic home background than pure bullies and pure victims.[16]

It is not yet clear why there is a higher proportion of bully-victims in primary than in post-primary school. While it may be that the pupils in lower grades may have different behavioural characteristics from those in the higher grades,[17] it may also be that pupils, as they grow older, become more discerning about what they assess as bullying and victimisation. We know, for example, that with age comes a greater understanding of the typical definition of bullying. It is possible, therefore, that bully-victims, as they gain self-awareness, may come to realise the inappropriateness of claiming victim status in view of their more impulsive and reactive aggressive style, as well as their propensity to bully physically.

How Common is Bullying?
In Ireland, in an average primary school class, there is likely to be at least three children who bully only and another three to four who are bully-victims. In an average post-primary class, we would expect to find two or three pure bullies and one or two bully-victims. (See Appendix for the percentages of victims, bullies and bully-victims from third class in primary school to sixth year in post-primary school.)

It is of note that over a ten-year period (1996–2006), while we have seen a decrease of children bullying others at primary level, there has been an increase at post-primary level from 10.8 per cent to 13.5 per cent.[18] Recent figures we have for cyber-bullying show that there are over three times as many teenagers involved in traditional bullying as there are in cyber-bullying.[19] Over two-thirds of cyber-bullies were also traditional bullies. Some are also traditional victims possibly using cyber tactics to get back at the 'bullies'. More boys than girls admit to cyber-bullying.

Bullying others decreases with age throughout primary school and into the first year of post-primary school. However, there is an increase in peer bullying, especially among boys, in second year of post-primary school, which does not decrease significantly until fifth year.[20]

Key Messages
- Bullying is a learned behaviour, with the home playing a critical role in the development of aggressive attitudes and behaviour.
- School children and adolescents who bully tend towards proactive/predatory rather than reactive aggression.
- Pupils who bully tend to be tough-minded, showing little remorse, empathy or concern for their victim's feelings. They may indeed argue that the victim deserves to be ill-treated.
- Bullying can be motivated by envy or jealousy, by boredom, or by competing for attention and social status, thus in the process satisfying needs to dominate and be in control. Bullying may also be a means by which to avoid victimisation, understanding that you are best served by getting your retaliation in first.
- Bullying can be symptomatic of a conduct disorder, which is more likely to be anti-social than neurotic in nature.
- A minority of children who bully are also victims. They are commonly referred to as bully-victims.
- Bully-victims tend to be easily provoked and frequently tease and provoke others.
- In essence, they are more socially inept and more reactively aggressive than pupils who bully only (pure bullies).

Notes

1. Rutter, M., Maughan, B., Mortimore, P., Ouston, J. and Smith, A., *Fourteen Thousand Hours: Secondary Schools and Their Effects on Children*, Cambridge: Harvard University Press, 1979.
2. Barlett, C.P. and Rodeheffer, C., 'Effects of Realism on Extended Violent and Nonviolent Video Game Play on Aggressive Thoughts, Feelings, and Physiological Arousal' in *Aggressive Behaviour*, 35 (2009), pp. 213–224.
3. Barlett, T., Branch, O., Rodeheffer, C. and Harris, R., 'How Long do the Short-term Violent Video Game Effects Last?' in *Aggressive Behaviour*, 35 (2009), pp. 125–236.
4. Fanti, K.A., Vanman, E., Heinrich, C.C. and Avraamides, M.N., 'Desensitization to Media Violence Over A Short Period of Time' in *Aggressive Behaviour*, 35 (2009), pp. 179–187.
5. Hogan, D., 'Victim of Bullying Too Afraid to Go to School', *Irish Times*, 11 March 1995.
6. Jackson, J.S., *Bye-Bye, Bully*, Indiana: Abbey Press, 2003.
7. Stephenson, P. and Smith, D., 'Bullying in the Junior School' in Tattum, D. and Lane, D.A., *Bullying in Schools*, Stoke-on-Trent: Trentham Books, 1989.

8. Pornari, C.D. and Wood, J., 'Peer and Cyber Aggression in Secondary School Students: The Role of Moral Disengagement, Hostile Attribution Bias, and Outcome Expectancies' in *Aggressive Behaviour*, 36 (2010), pp. 81–94.

9. O'Moore, M. and Kirkham, C. 'The Relationship Between Bullying and Self-Esteem' in *Aggressive Behaviour*, 27 (2001), pp. 269–283.

10. Smith, P.K., 'Cyber-Bullying – Learning from the Past, Looking to the Future' in *Book of Abstracts: Cyber-Bullying: Definition and Measurement*, Cost Action 1So85 Workshop, Mykolas Rameris University, Vilnius, Lithuania, 22–23 August, 2009.

11. Connolly, I. and O'Moore, M., 'Personality and Family Relations of Children who Bully' in *Personality and Individual Differences*, 35 (2002), pp. 559–567.

12. Olweus, D., *Bullying at School: What We Know and What We Can Do*, Oxford: Blackwell, 1993.

13. O'Moore, A.M., 'Teachers Hold the Key to Change' in Elliot, M. (ed.), *Bullying: A Practical Guide to Coping for Schools*, 3rd Edition, London: Pearson Education, 2002.

14. O'Moore, M and Minton, S.J., *Bullying, Cyber-Bullying, Gender and Personality*, 2002. Submitted for publication.

15. Cook, C.R., Williams, K.R., Guerra, N.G., Kim, T.E. and Sadek, S., 'Predictors of Bullying and Victimization in Childhood and Adolescence: A Meta-analytic Investigation' in *School Psychology Quarterly*, 25 (2010), pp. 65–83.

16. Unnever, J.D., 'Bullies, Aggressive Victims and Victims: Are they Distinct Groups?' in *Aggressive Behaviour*, 31 (2005), pp. 153–171.

17. Solberg, M.E., 'Bullies and Victims at School: Are They the Same Pupils?' in *British Journal of Educational Psychology*, 77 (2007), pp. 441–464.

18. Minton, S.J. and O'Moore, M., 'The Effectiveness of a Nationwide Intervention Programme to Prevent and Counter School Bullying in Ireland' in *International Journal of Psychology and Psychology Therapy*, 8 (2008), pp. 1–12.

19. O'Moore, A.M. and Minton, S.J., 'Cyber-Bullying: The Irish Experience' in Quin, C. and Tawse, S. (eds), *Handbook of Aggressive Behavior Research*, Hauppauge, NY: Nova Science Publishers, Inc., 2009.

20. O'Moore, M., Kirkham, C. and Smith, M., 'Bullying Behaviour in Irish Schools: A Nationwide Study' in *Irish Journal of Psychology*, 18.2 (1997).

5

WHAT ARE THE CONSEQUENCES OF VICTIMISATION AND BULLYING?

> I was bullied 25 years ago. Why after so long am I still feeling the ill effects of it? ... I've struggled to keep the dark images of being bullied locked away but no matter how hard I try, I'm still haunted, still effected, still angry.[1]

These sentiments expressed by filmmaker Eamonn Devlin are not unusual and I have yet to meet an adult who is not emotionally affected in some way by having been bullied at school. Generally, their feelings are still very raw, so it is not difficult to imagine how they felt while it was occurring. The extreme hurt and humiliation that they suffered as a child or teenager seems to cling to them. Their memories have the power to put them down again and again. Their anger is also palpable, which explains why some actually find themselves years later taking out their anger in some revengeful action against the perpetrator should they happen to meet one another on a chance occasion. For example, one man told me how he was away on business and before calling it a day he had gone to a pub to have a drink. Standing at the counter with his pint in hand he heard someone further along the counter call out his name. He turned around and recognised the person as one who had targeted him in school. He went over to him and on hearing, 'How are you doing?' he surprised himself by tipping his pint over his former tormentor's head.

Since *The Star* reported[2] on the results of my first study of school bullying,[3] I received a steady flow of phone calls, letters and e-mails, which detailed the anguish and despair suffered by children and their families as a result of bullying and violence within their school community. The Anti-Bullying Centre (www.abc.tcd.ie), which I launched in 1996, continues to receive calls from individuals seeking either help for themselves or for their children. Over the years I have therefore gathered a very rich source of anecdotal information on the ramifications of being bullied. The most common effects are:

- Stress
- Reduced ability to concentrate
- Lack of motivation and energy
- Poor or deteriorating school work
- Anxiety about going to school
- Loss of confidence and self-esteem
- Lack of appetite or comfort eating
- Depression
- Aggressive eruptions/tantrums
- Withdrawn, unhappy demeanour
- Feeling isolated, betrayed, hopeless
- Development of nervous 'tics', stammering/stuttering
- Sleeping problems, bedwetting, nightmares
- Headache, stomach/bowel problems
- Alcohol/drug/substance abuse
- Panic attacks
- Self-harming
- Attempted suicide/suicide.

If you have heard a victim speak of their current or past experience of bullying, you will undoubtedly have been struck by the rawness and intensity of emotion and how the experience only seemed like yesterday. I have found that interviews with public figures, such as broadcasters, actors and sports stars, to be a source of considerable comfort to targeted individuals who have not achieved closure on their experience of bullying. To hear especially that big personalities had big problems at school makes many feel less ashamed and less alone. For the first time they may come to realise that the symptoms they have suffered, and may still be suffering, are not peculiar to them. Instead, they might begin to grasp that their feelings about being bullied were normal, and that their being targeted said more about the person who bullied than it did about them.

A case in point would be Derek Davis, who as a television personality would, to many, be regarded as an unlikely target of bullying, yet he was pushed to the brink of a nervous breakdown. In his own words he stated, 'You feel useless and inadequate and if somebody keeps calling you a fat, useless lump, then that reinforces a very poor self-image.' He believes that having 'a rotten self-image' while trying to deal with the demands of the middle teen years can make you 'become absolutely desperate'.[4]

While individuals may find anecdotal information helpful, professionals and policymakers tend to seek scientific evidence so that they can more accurately manage reform and develop policy.

Below I hope to give a taste of the scientific evidence that highlights the pattern of distress that is caused by bullying. I have arranged it so that the reader can get a sense of both the short- and long-term effects on physical health and mental well-being that being bullied or bullying others can have.

The Effects of Being Bullied on Physical Health

A study carried out on primary school children in England showed that children who were bullied at school suffered from more common health symptoms than did non-bullied children. Katrina Williams and her co-researchers[5] found, for example, that quite apart from feeling sad, the victimised children reported not sleeping well, bed-wetting and suffering from occasional headaches and stomach aches.

A study in Ireland, which I was involved in, that was carried out by a fifth-year medical student[6] for his paediatric project, showed that primary school children who were victimised were nearly twice as likely to miss school through illness and twice as likely to visit their General Practitioners than were non-bullied children. The children who were bullied were three times more likely to get headaches once a week or more often, and, like their counterparts in the UK, they felt sad once a week or more frequently.

The findings from the World Health Organisation's international study on health behaviour in school children aged eleven, thirteen and fifteen, carried out from 2001–2002, found that victims experience subjective health complaints more often and report poorer self-rated health and lower levels of life satisfaction than those not involved in bullying. It is of note that the study also found that nearly 80 per cent of fifteen-year-olds who reported negative school experiences reported multiple recurrent subjective health complaints, and 37 per cent reported smoking frequently. Girls were found to report lower levels of positive health outcomes than boys across all age groups.[7]

The Effects of Being Bullied on Mental Well-Being

Sadness, loneliness, fear and anger are the emotions most commonly found to be associated with being bullied. This cannot be better illustrated than by Elaine Doyle, who, speaking at a conference about her victimisation while at secondary school, had this to say:

> I was so confused, angry, upset and my mood was constantly changing that even a simple 'good morning' would send me straight into a tantrum. It was a very hard time for my family. I became the daughter and sister out of hell, locking myself in my room, screaming at them, running away from the house. I started drinking very heavily when I went out at weekends, and also thought of taking my own life on numerous occasions ... to me it was taking the easy way out. I reached the stage where I believed I was the problem and that everyone would be better off if I was gone. I also felt that nobody would notice I was gone or even miss me.[8]

In our most recent study on cyber-bullying,[9] four-fifths of the teenagers sampled reported negative emotions as a result of being cyber-victims, with as many feeling upset as they felt angry. A sizable proportion also felt afraid.

Reading a testimony by John Halligan,[10] where he connects cyber-bullying with his son's suicide, leaves one in no doubt about the potential ill-effects of cyber-bullying. While he recognises that his son, 'a sweet, gentle and lanky thirteen-year-old', was not 'the first boy in history to be bullied and have his heart crushed by a pretty girl's rejection', he came to recognise when he discovered the tactics that had been used by the peers that 'technology was being utilised as a weapon far more effective and far reaching than the simple tools' that he had as a kid. He believes his son would have survived the traditional forms of bullying, but that 'there are few of us who would have had the resilience and stamina to sustain such a nuclear attack on our feelings and reputation as a young teen in the midst of rapid physical and emotional changes and raging hormones'.

Poor self-esteem has consistently been found to characterise children and adolescents who are victimised. For example, our Irish study[11] showed that victims from age eight to eighteen, compared to those who had not reported being bullied, had greater feelings of inadequacy in all the domains of self-esteem. The domains of self-esteem that were examined by the Piers Harris Self-Concept Test were happiness and satisfaction, popularity, anxiety, physical appearance and attributes, intellectual and school status and behaviour. As the frequency of bullying increased, so did the effect it had on each of the self-concept domains. Not surprisingly, the victims suffered the lowest levels of self-esteem, reported a greater dislike of school and had the fewest friends.

Depression, thoughts of suicide and suicide are increasingly recognised as being strongly associated with being bullied in childhood and adolescence.[12] The diary of Irish schoolgirl, Leanne Wolfe, broadcast on RTÉ,[13] is a stark reminder of this. Also close to home is the tragic death of Megan Gillan by overdose,[14] who had been targeted by her tormentors on a social networking site. Most recently we learnt of the tragic death by suicide in Massachusetts of the Irish schoolgirl, Phoebe Prince, who was a victim of vicious high school stalking and bullying, a lot of it carried out in cyberspace.[15]

As a link exists between school absenteeism, bullying and depression, it would be advisable for all teachers, when faced with school absenteeism, to check if bullying may be a possible cause. To simply ask the pupils in question whether or not they are being bullied may not be sufficient in view of the very strong reluctance to tell. It may be necessary to shadow the child as well as be alert to the tell-tale signs of being bullied. As teacher support can have a strong influence on the self-concept of pupils, it can act also as a buffer against the negative impact of peer victimisation and so reduce the level of emotional and physical complaints associated with victimisation.[16]

Children's understanding of why they have been targeted has been found to affect the degree to which they suffer the ill effects.[17] If they perceive that the reason for being bullied is due to some personal fault, weakness or deficiency that is outside of their control and, therefore, cannot be changed, they are more likely to experience greater anxiety, depression and decreased self-esteem than if they were to find someone or something else to blame, such as being in the wrong place at the wrong time. It follows from this that children who receive negative feedback from their peers, teachers, parents and others can so easily believe that there truly is something wrong with them. To be continually referred to as, for example, 'egg head', 'bat ears', 'reject', 'brat' or 'weirdo' can be extremely damaging to one's self-esteem.

Because social relationships and support play such a major role in the development of self-esteem, it is not surprising that the feeling of sadness, loneliness, isolation and rejection that victims experience substantially affects their self-image. Low self-esteem coupled with feelings of shame, guilt, loss of identity, lack of confidence, self-blame or being blamed by others – all often felt by victims – can so easily lead to a sense of hopelessness.

In the absence of effective parent and teacher intervention, it is the feeling of hopelessness or the feeling of there being 'no light at the end of the tunnel' that can so easily cause depression among victims of bullying and very sadly lead to self-harm or suicide.

Long-Term Effects of Victimisation

It has been found that the poor self-esteem that so often results from being bullied in childhood can have long-term consequences, so that adulthood becomes marred by poor levels of self-esteem and depression. Generally, the duration of a child's victimisation will determine the magnitude of the adjustment difficulties.

A study of college students[18] in the USA found that the effects of bullying were worse for those who were victimised for the first time late on in puberty, with female students more likely to react aggressively when provoked, while male students tended to turn to alcohol to escape bad situations.

On following over six thousand Finnish children, it was found that to be bullied at age eight was associated with a wide range of psychological problems at age sixteen, which resulted in the referral to child mental health services.[19] To be bullied in the early teen years increased the risk of psychiatric symptoms, and when the information about frequent victimisation and bullying was used as a screening test, it identified that over a quarter of those victims developed a psychiatric disorder within ten to fifteen years.[20] A much quoted study showing long-term adverse effects of bullying is that of Gilmartin, who drew the conclusion that boys who are severely bullied at school by their peers are at risk of becoming 'love shy' and, as a result, are more likely to have difficulties forming intimate relationships.[21]

Effects on Learning and Education

An unwillingness to attend school has also been long associated with victimisation. Children who are victimised are unable to draw maximum benefit from teaching and learning because so much of their energy is taken up with trying to keep safe. Importantly, fear of future physical assault has been found to cause the greatest anxiety.[22]

It should also be said that care must also be taken to ensure that children and young people do not feel victimised in any way by school staff, as the emotional impact can be even greater than that caused by peer victimisation. Researchers who have looked into student victimisation by school staff have found that the use of physical, emotional and sexual victimisation by staff can severely threaten pupils' sense of safety, sense of trust towards adults and long-term emotional well-being.[23]

The Consequences of Engaging in Bullying Behaviour

In Relation to General Health

According to the World Health Organisation study referred to earlier, 'bullies' reported their general health to be not as good as that of their counterparts who had not bullied others. More girls than boys who bullied were adversely affected.

In Relation to Mental Health

It may be surprising to learn that it is not only victims of bullying who risk depression and thoughts of suicide. This is also true of children and adolescents who engage in bullying behaviour. Indeed, it has been claimed that the greatest risk of suicidal ideation was detected among the youngsters who bullied.[24]

Depressive symptoms among boys and girls who bully have also been reported by researchers in Norway. However, there is still some uncertainty as to the role of depressive symptoms in bullying behaviour. The research found that when the level of depressive symptoms increased, especially among the girls who bullied, so too did the level of power-related proactive aggression directed at the victim.[25]

In view of the strong interaction that is evident between depression and bullying, it follows that every effort should be made to reduce depression among boys and girls in the hope that it will also reduce their bullying behaviour.

Long-Term Consequences of Bullying Others

Bullying others throughout childhood and adolescence is associated with an increased risk of developing an anti-social personality, as well as depressive and anxiety disorders. It also heightens the likelihood of drug abuse and lawbreaking behaviour in adulthood. Occupational and educational attainment has also been found to suffer.[26]

Bullying in childhood has also been found to lead to violence in dating. Obviously the tendency to exert power is carried over to relationships with the opposite sex[27] and perhaps to parenting. There is also evidence to suggest that girls who bully in childhood will develop an aggressive parenting style.

With the evidence that has been available to us so far, it seems clear that early aggression is a strong predictor of later aggression and that bullying behaviour is an early warning sign of long-term behavioural difficulties.

The Effects of Being Both Bullied and of Bullying Others (Bully-Victims)

There is less specific data relating to the ill-effects of being a bully-victim, as it is only quite recently that bully-victims have come to be regarded as a distinct group. However, the evidence that is available points to them having greater psychological problems than either victims or bullies. Whereas victims tend to suffer from anxiety disorders and bullies tend to suffer from conduct disorders that are anti-social in nature, bully-victims are affected by both social and emotional disorders. As their behaviours cause them to be more isolated and rejected by their peers than either victims or bullies, it is not surprising that they tend to dislike school and, as a result, have a high rate of absenteeism.

The more frequently the bullies are victimised, the lower their global self-esteem and the greater their feeling of inadequacy in relation to the individual domains of self-esteem, which I mentioned earlier. They also suffer from depression to a greater extent than pure victims and pure bullies.[28]

The Long-Term Effects for Bully-Victims

The outcome for bully-victims is stark when one takes the Finnish longitudinal study into account. It found that 30 per cent of children who were bully-victims had a psychiatric disorder on follow up. This compared to 18 per cent who were bullies only and 17 per cent who were victims only. When the bully-victims were compared to children who had not been involved in bullying either as victim or bully, it was further found that the bully-victims had a five-fold increased risk of developing a psychiatric disorder. So significant were the findings that the authors concluded that a screening strategy would be more cost effective than universal screening to identify psychiatric disorders.

Consequences for Bystanders

Increasingly, we are recognising that bystanders to bullying also suffer physical and emotional symptoms. They become especially anxious and fearful and, as a result, they develop a dislike for school.

They worry that they may be drawn into bullying because of peer pressure. Others feel that if they don't join in they may be rejected by their peer group. As one student in our nationwide study stated: 'I have joined in once or twice. It's just if everyone else is I join in cause I don't want to feel left out.' Others join in because they worry that they may become the next victim, as the following comment illustrates: 'If I thought the person that was bullying was going to bully me, I might stick up for the person that was bullying.'

Guilt is also an emotion that troubles bystanders and this can stay with them right through their adulthood. For example, this is what one bystander had to say:

I am writing this report as a victim of bullying in a different sense – victims suffer, I suffer from an overwhelming sense of guilt. I am a spectator, the one who stands, looks, sees but never intervenes. Of course I feel guilty. I mean, this is really conscience-striking stuff. What can I do?

If I say anything would it make a difference or would it make it worse? Can I risk it? Is it worth it? Would I become the victim that I pity? Take, for example, a case of isolation or loneliness. I say that I feel sorry for that person, but do I go out of my way to talk to them to encourage them to sit beside me? The answer is NO, so I'm a hypocrite. Isn't that a reason to isolate or bully me? At least I'd stand up for myself better than them – or would I? I put myself apart from the so-called bullies but I'm no better myself. The mass rules, the majority is OK. We all have to fit in, try to blend, be the same and never stand out. I can imagine some of the pain they hide even though it must hit them inside and eat them raw. It scares me how easy it could have happened to me.[29]

We know from our nationwide study that it is the children with the highest self-esteem who reported that 'they would try and help in some way' when they saw someone of their own age being bullied. However, children can be trained to become better defenders and this is something which I will address later. In view of the strong evidence that places children and teens at serious risk of physical and mental ill health, as well as educational and vocational underachievement, it is critical that no effort should be spared in trying to prevent and counter bullying. How this can best be done is something I will address in the next two parts of the book.

Key Messages
- Aggression in childhood is a predictor of a wide range of difficulties in adult life, including marital difficulties, health problems, anti-social and criminal behaviour, lower levels of occupational attainment and educational achievement.
- Aggression in childhood and adolescence is a warning sign of bullying behaviour.

- Children involved in bullying, either as bully, victim or bully-victim, are at risk of developing health problems and psychosocial difficulties.
- Victims are especially at risk of anxiety, sadness, loneliness, low self-esteem, depression, physical illness, school refusal, educational underachievement, self-harm, thoughts of suicide, suicidal attempts and even suicide.
- Bullies are particularly at risk of later aggressive, anti-social and criminal behaviour. They are also prone to depressive illness and suicidal ideation.
- Bully-victims are especially at risk of all the ill effects associated with being bullied as well as those of bullying others. Thus, they are affected the worst mentally and physically out of all those involved in bullying.
- Bystanders can become anxious and fearful and can suffer feelings of guilt, sometimes lasting a lifetime.

Notes

1. Eamonn Devlin, *Bully for You*, Triplevision Productions Ltd., broadcast on BBC (NI), September 2008.
2. Moloney, S., 'Victims in our Schools', *The Star*, 4 October 1989.
3. O'Moore, A.M. and Hillery, B., 'Bullying in Dublin Schools' in *Irish Journal of Psychology*, 10 (1989), pp. 426–441.
4. Walshe, J., 'Big Personality, Big Problems', *Irish Independent*, 24 October 1994.
5. Williams, K., Chambers, M., Logan, S. and Robinson, D., 'Association of Common Health Symptoms with Bullying in Primary School Children' in *British Medical Journal*, 313 (1996), pp. 17–19.
6. Canavan, J., 'Bullying and Health in Primary School Children: Is There an Association?', unpublished fifth-year medical project, Department of Paediatrics, Trinity College Dublin.
7. World Health Organisation, *Young People's Health in Context: Health Behaviour in School-aged Children (HBSC) Study, Intermediate Report from 2001/2002 Survey*, Health Policy for Children and Adolescents, No. 4, 2004.
8. Doyle, E., 'Buying Time' in *Proceedings of the Second National Conference on Bullying and Suicide in Schools*, The Association of Suicidology and the National Suicide Review Group, Tralee, 28–29 November 2002.
9. O'Moore, A.M. and Minton, S.J., 'Cyber-Bullying: The Irish Experience' in Quin, C. and Tawse, S. (eds), *Handbook of Aggressive Behavior Research*, Hauppauge, NY: Nova Science Publishers, Inc., 2009.
10. Halligan, J. 'Foreword' in Kowalski, R.M., Limber, S.P. and Agatston, P.W. (eds), *Cyber-Bullying: Bullying in the Digital Age*, Oxford: Blackwell, 2008.
11. O'Moore, M. and Kirkham, C., 'The Relationship Between Bullying and Self-Esteem' in *Aggressive Behaviour*, 27 (2001), pp. 269–283.

12. Lawlor, M., 'School Bullying Costs' in *Irish Psychiatrist*, 7 (2006), pp. 111–115.

13. The Diary of Leanne Wolfe, RTÉ Radio 1: Documentary on One, 2008: www. rte. ie/radio1/doconone.

14. 'Victims of Cyber-Bullying Talk', *The Sun*, 6 August 2009.

15. Lynch, D., 'Bullied to Death', *Sunday Independent*, 14 March 2010.

16. Holmquist, K., 'Bullying in Ireland: Schools are in Denial', *Irish Times Weekend Review*, 18 September 2010.

17. Graham, S. and Juvonen, J., 'An Attributional Approach to Peer Victimisation' in Juvonen, J. and Graham, S. (eds), *Peer Harassment in School: The Plight of the Vulnerable and Victimised*, New York: Guilford Press, 2001.

18. Philips, H., 'Effects of Bullying Worse for Teens', *New Scientist*, 29 October 2004.

19. Sourander, A., Helsteln, L., Helenius, H. and Piha, J., 'Persistence of Bullying from Childhood to Adolescence – A Longitudinal 8-Year Follow-up Study' in *Child Abuse and Neglect*, 24 (2000), pp. 873–881.

20. Sourander, A., et al., 'What is the Early Adulthood Outcome of Boys Who Bully or Are Bullied in Childhood?', Finnish 'From a Boy to a Man' study, in *Pediatrics*, 120 (2007), pp. 397–404.

21. Gilmartin, B.G., 'Peer Group Antecedents of Sever Love-Shyness in Males' in *Journal of Personality*, 55 (1987), pp. 459–467.

22. Boulton, M.J., Trueman, M. and Murray, L., 'Associations Between Peer Victimisation, Fear of Future Victimisation and Disrupted Concentration on Class Work Among Junior School Pupils' in *British Journal of Educational Psychology*, 78.3 (2008), pp. 473–489.

23. Khoury-Kassabri, M., Astor, R.A. and Benbenishty, R., 'Student Victimisation by School Staff in the Context of an Israeli National School Safety Campaign' in *Aggressive Behaviour*, 34 (2008), pp. 1–8.

24. Kaltialo-Heino, R., Rimpelo, M., Martunen, M., Rimpela, A. and Rantenau, P., 'Bullying, Depression and Suicidal Ideation in Finnish Adolescents: School Survey' in *British Medical Journal*, 319 (1999), pp. 348–351.

25. Roland, E., 'Aggression, Depression and Bullying Others' in *Aggressive Behaviour*, 28 (2002), pp. 198–206.

26. Huesman, L.R, Dubow, E.F. and Boxer, P., 'Continuity of Aggression from Childhood to Early Adulthood as a Predictor of Life Outcomes' in *Aggressive Behaviour*, 35 (2009), pp. 136–149.

27. Connolly, J., Pepler, D., Craig. W. and Taradash, A., 'Dating Experiences of Bullies in Early Adolescence' in *Child Development*, 5 (2000), pp. 299–310.

28. Nansel, T.R., Craig, W., Overpeck, M.D., Saluja, G. and Ruan, W.J., 'Cross-national Consistency in the Relationship Between Bullying Behaviours and Psychosocial Adjustment' in *Archives of Paediatrics and Adolescent Medicine*, 158 (2004), pp. 730–736.

29. Report compiled by Heather Jones, *Our Times*, Wesley College, December 1994.

PART TWO

6 | HOW SCHOOLS CAN PREVENT AND DEAL WITH BULLYING

While there are many schools and parents who are taking effective action to deal with aggression, bullying and violence, there are many who are still uncertain about what steps to take. The next two parts of this book aim to remove the uncertainty and provide solutions that are grounded in best practice to prevent and counter school bullying.

Given the potentially serious effects of victimisation and bullying on children's physical and mental health and educational achievement, it is clear that schools have a role to play in the prevention and intervention of school bullying. How this can be best achieved will be the focus of this part of the book.

David Farrington, an eminent professor of psychological criminology at the Institute of Criminology, Cambridge, together with Maria Ttofi, conducted a recent rigorous and systematic review of the effectiveness of existing anti-bullying programmes.[1] Most importantly, he found that school-based programmes proved to be effective in reducing bullying and victimisation among school-going children. The duration and intensity of the programmes were, as might be expected, significantly associated with a decrease in both bully and victim problems. The programme components that were found to be most effective in reducing the level of bullying were as follows:

- Anti-bullying policy
- Disciplinary methods
- Playground supervision
- Teacher training
- Classroom rules
- Classroom management
- School conferences
- Information for parents

- Parent training/meetings
- Co-operative group work (between teacher and experts from other disciplines).

The key elements in reducing the level of victimisation were:

- Parent training/meetings
- Videos
- Disciplinary methods
- Cooperative group work
- Playground supervision.

All these elements can be captured by what is now commonly referred to as the 'whole school approach to bullying prevention', a strategy that was introduced by Dan Olweus and Erling Roland in response to bullying-related suicides in Norway. It should be noted that Farrington and Ttofi found that the total number of elements and the duration and intensity of the programme made for the greatest decrease in bullying and victimisation.

What is Meant by a Whole School Approach to Bullying Prevention?

A whole school approach to bullying takes responsibility for both bullying prevention and intervention by the entire school community giving it a high priority. Because the strategies extend to all the members of the school community – staff, students, parents and others associated with the school (bus drivers, traffic wardens, local shop keepers) – the approach is increasingly referred to as a 'whole school community approach'.

The most important aspect of a whole school community approach to bullying is the publication of a well-designed policy. Other key elements include:

- exercises to raise awareness of bullying among teachers, students, parents and representatives of the community to which the school belongs;
- encouraging students, with the help of curriculum and extra-curricular activities, to play a greater role in stopping, helping and telling when they witness incidents of bullying behaviour;

- improving the monitoring and supervision of students, especially in playgrounds.

At the heart of a whole school approach lie values, beliefs and attitudes that are shared by the whole school community. No longer is taking a stand against bullying associated with individual teachers, pupils or parents, but rather it is the responsibility of all members of the school community. All know what is expected of them and are aware of the consequences should their behaviour fall short of the standards that have been set. I will now outline how this can be achieved.

Begin with Developing an Anti-Bullying Policy

It is to be expected that most schools in Ireland and Northern Ireland will have an anti-bullying policy that is either a 'stand-alone' policy or an integral part of their Code of Behaviour and Discipline, as recommended by the Department of Education and Skills, or in Northern Ireland as part of their Pastoral Care Policies. Either way, an anti-bullying policy provides a framework for how to deal with bullying. Most importantly, it provides schools with a valuable opportunity to communicate to all its members where the school stands on the issue of bullying and how it intends to deal with it.

It is clear, however, from the many calls that are made by parents, teachers and others to our helpline, which forms part of the work of the Anti-Bullying Research and Resource Centre (ABC), founded in Trinity College Dublin in 1996, that individual schools vary enormously in the way they develop and implement their anti-bullying policies. It is to be expected, therefore, that there are many schools throughout Ireland, both north and south, that would benefit from a review of their policies. Even if there are schools that currently pride themselves on having a good policy, best practice would be that they review it regularly in order to take new developments on board.

The Process for Developing an Anti-Bullying Policy

Ideally, an anti-bullying policy should serve the whole school community. It is vital, therefore, that all in the school community feel that they have had a say in the development of the policy. Increasingly, people are touchy about having what they see as yet more new rules and regulations imposed upon them, whereas they are more content to endorse a policy that they themselves have had a part in developing. Also, when they are given a voice they are more likely to develop a sense of ownership and a shared understanding of the school's expectations. Most importantly, however, they will be less inclined to flout what they themselves have had a hand in designing and agreeing upon, thus consultation is the key to a successful policy.

Who to Consult?

To arrive at a policy that meets the needs of the school community, all the members need to be consulted by means of questionnaires or focus groups. By 'school community' I mean students, parents and all staff, teaching and non-teaching (canteen staff, grounds staff and caretakers). School bus drivers, traffic wardens and local shopkeepers can also make valuable contributions to an anti-bullying policy.

To achieve the most informed responses from the school community a range of exercises to raise awareness may be necessary. This will allow the school community to develop a greater understanding of the subject. It is only when there is a deeper understanding of bullying and the strategies that have been shown to reduce it that ambitious and progressive views can be expected from the members of the community.

To consult with the individual groups (i.e. staff, parents and students) who represent the school community and arrange sessions to raise awareness may seem very labour intensive and cumbersome . However, the rewards will outweigh any imposition that the process may cause. We should be reminded strongly of the World Health Organisation's viewpoint that upward investment brings downstream results.

Who Manages the Change?

The principal, under the direction of the Board of Management, will have the responsibility for effecting a change in policy. Principals are key in effecting change, as they are in the strongest position to influence attitudes and to set and uphold standards.

However, principals may choose to appoint a Policy Development Team, which is made up of representatives from the different groups

as the new way to deal with acts of bullying. (See Chapters 7 and 11 for details on co-operative learning structures and restorative approaches respectively.)

9) *Launching the policy.* For the policy to reach as wide an audience as possible and have maximum impact, a well-planned launch with a celebratory tone would be desirable. This can take the style of any other awareness-raising campaign. For example, there can be displays of the students' work that may have formed part of the awareness-raising activities in preparation for the policy development, for example, art work, posters, poetry, music, film, drama, and so on. To reach out to people beyond the launch requires plans to be made to publish the policy on the school website, in the school prospectus and in the students' journal. A charter that summarises all the elements within the policy should also be posted around the school (see p. 101 for an example of a charter developed by students).

10) *Keeping the policy alive.* It is essential to keep the policy alive, leaving no room for complacency. School assemblies provide an ideal opportunity to reinforce the anti-bullying policy. Posters around the school should be regularly changed to attract attention. Other work arising from curriculum activities, for example, art, sculpture and poetry, should also be displayed around the school. Students can carry out surveys at a class-, year- or whole-school level as part of a mathematics lesson. Feedback of the results will reinforce the commitment to the policy, especially if students are given the task to review and revise anti-bullying codes that are specific to their class. Teachers should also hold regular meetings to share experiences on bully/victim problems in order to learn from each other's successes and failures.

11) *Reviewing, revising and renewing the policy.* It is only by reviewing the policy regularly, ideally once a year, that a school can expect ongoing improvements in the reduction of bullying. The responsibility for the evaluation can lie with the anti-bullying committee. Feedback should ideally be sought from staff (teaching and non-teaching), students, parents and other representatives of the school community. Aspects to examine would be:

- The level of bullying as reflected by a survey and the number of incidents reported to staff
- The level of enrolments and exits from school by students and staff
- The level of absenteeism
- The general working environment – a pleasing environment encourages positive behaviour
- The level of peer support or positive pupil-led strategies.

There is an auditing tool designed by a former school principal, George Varnava,[2] which can assist schools greatly in keeping on top of their continuing efforts to promote a bully-free climate in their schools. It is called 'Checkpoints for Schools' and consists of six checkpoints: home, school and community; values; organisation; environment; curriculum; training. Each of these six checkpoints consists of ten statements, which relate to different aspects of school life, examples being: 'Vulnerable and aggressive students are identified early and supportive strategies devised to pre-empt difficulty. Students themselves and, as appropriate, parents are involved'; 'Good relationships are consistently fostered, and all adults model non-violent behaviour'; 'Violent language, the violent use of language and name-calling are consistently discouraged'. A tick is placed against each of the statements indicating whether the statement represents what is in place, what is proposed or what is not in place. The results are then transferred to a web, which illustrates visually the stage reached by the school in addressing bullying and highlights where further action needs to be taken. For any school wishing to carry out an audit, I recommend that they consult Chris Gittin's book, *Violence Reduction in Schools: How to Make a Difference*.[3] Within it they will find a most useful chapter titled 'Finding out More', written by Peter Galvin, a senior educational psychologist.[4]

What Goes into an Anti-Bullying Policy?

An anti-bullying policy should be regarded as a generalised response to bullying. It should provide comprehensive principles and guidelines but it cannot be expected to detail procedures and practices in such a way that can cover all eventualities; schools will, on occasion, need some flexibility. However, there is now general agreement that the following features should be included in a policy.

1) A statement of purpose. The policy needs to state its purpose. This should be straightforward in view of the fact that schools have a duty of care towards students and staff and, therefore, it will need to take all reasonable measures to ensure that the school is a safe place for both students and staff. Reference can be made to Ireland's own Health and Safety Act and to the United Nations Charter for Children's Rights, which makes it very clear that every child has the right to a stimulating learning environment that is free from humiliation, oppression and abuse. The policy can then further stress the expectations that it has of its members in assisting the school to prevent and counter bullying in an effort to make it safe for them all. For example, the expectations inherent in our ABC whole school community approach to bullying prevention,[5] and which make up its abbreviation 'ABC', is that the school community will 'Avoid aggression', 'Be tolerant' and 'Care for others'.

2) A definition of bullying. Explicit reference should be made to all forms of bullying (verbal, physical, social, sexual and cyber-bullying). It is highly recommended that policies include and also give examples of the forms of bullying that have their basis in discrimination and prejudice (racial, sexist, sexual, transgender and homophobic). This will avoid drawing up separate policies when abusive and hurtful behaviour is common to all forms of bullying and will require similar forms of intervention.

3) The negative impact of bullying for both victims and bullies. Reference should be made to the cost of bullying to the victim and to the perpetrator, as this will help to dispel the many misconceptions that surround bullying. It will also strengthen the grounds to vigorously pursue an anti-bullying policy.

4) The signs of bullying. Some inclusion should be made to the warning signs of bullying (for example, changes in behaviour, work performance and attendance) because it points to the importance of noticing changes in a student's behaviour as a result of bullying.

5) The policy aims. Mention should be made of what the school hopes to achieve. It is difficult to improve on the Policy Aims as recommended in the National Guidelines for Countering Bullying Behaviour in Primary and Post-Primary School (DES, 1993). These are as follows:

99

- To create a school ethos that encourages children to disclose and discuss incidents of bullying behaviour.
- To raise awareness of bullying as a form of unacceptable behaviour with school management, teachers, pupils, parents/guardians.
- To ensure comprehensive supervision and monitoring measures through which all areas of school activity are kept under observation.
- To develop procedures for investigating and dealing with incidents of bullying behaviour.
- To develop a programme of support for those affected by bullying behaviour and for those involved in bullying behaviour.
- To work with and through the various local agencies in countering all forms of bullying and anti-social behaviour.
- To evaluate the effectiveness of school policy on anti-bullying behaviour.

6) *Prevention strategies.* Students, staff, parents and other representatives of the school community must be made aware that they all have a responsibility to:

- avoid engaging in bullying behaviour;
- discourage and intervene when you witness bullying behaviour;
- assist and give support to those targeted;
- report incidents.

In the Information Box below I have listed some key points to discuss with students in order to heighten their awareness of bullying and the stance that the school intends to take on it.

Information Box: Talking to Students about Bullying
Key points to put across:
- What bullying is and the different forms that it can take.
- That bullying is, and is seen in this school, as an unacceptable form of behaviour.
- That we all have a responsibility to contribute to a positive environment and safeguard the well-being of others.
- That if we are bullied, or know someone else being bullied, we try to stop it or report it to a member of staff.
- That violent retaliation will make things worse in the long run.
- Everyone has the right to equal treatment and respect regardless of any personal difference.

In addition, the school should specify the curricular activities that they have adopted to address attitudes, promote knowledge and understanding and provide opportunities for developing skills that can help to prevent bullying. School Council activities and peer support strategies (see Chapter 12) should also be promoted. It would be most effective if School Councils were given the task of developing a School Charter, which could be posted up in hallways and classrooms as a reminder to all students not to get involved in bullying. Below is an example of a School Charter.

Sample School Charter:
- Every child has the right to enjoy his/her learning and leisure FREE from bullying, both in the school and in the surrounding community.
- Our school community will NOT tolerate any bullying, even if the unkind actions were not intended to hurt.
- Pupils should support each other by reporting ALL instances of bullying.
- Bullying will be dealt with SERIOUSLY. We are a Telling School. Bullying is too serious not to report.

(Anti-Bullying Centre, Trinity College Dublin)

---

7) Procedures for reporting and investigating bullying. All members of the school community should be made aware of how they should go about reporting an incident of bullying and to whom they should report it. Procedures for investigating an incident should also be described. For example, it should be specified who will have the responsibility for investigating complaints of bullying (for example, the anti-bullying co-ordinator or year head) and who will report on the findings.

8) Intervention strategies for dealing with bullying. A description should be given of the intervention strategies that are available to the school. These may include curriculum approaches, restorative approaches (the 'Common Concern Method' and the 'No Blame Approach'), peer support strategies, mediation, counselling, aggression replacement training (ART) and sanctions, ranging from a verbal reprimand to suspension and expulsion.

9) Monitoring and evaluating the policy. An undertaking should be given to review the policy on a regular basis. An audit or needs analysis may be conducted for this purpose. This will help to keep the policy active while at the same time provide valuable information on the level of victimisation and bullying and where it takes place. This will allow also for the Board of Management to reward successes and encourage any renewing efforts that may be necessary to prevent and reduce further the level of bullying in evidence.

A Special Note

From an evaluation of anti-bullying policies in schools in Wales,[6] it is worth noting that the strongest policies were those which demonstrated the following key characteristics:

- The provision of very clear definitions of bullying, in particular those that acknowledge abuse of power as a criterion of bullying.
- A range of different types of bullying identified, which takes the reader beyond the more global definitions.
- In some schools, whole school policies and practices are clearly delineated as anti-bullying. In others they are embedded in other sets of initiatives. The latter policies were particularly strong where parental involvement was included at all stages.
- Mechanisms for pupil involvement ranged from direct to indirect reporting of bullying to preventative measures, including 'buddying' and mentoring processes.
- In the strongest policies, clear procedures were presented for staff, pupils and parents, with the best providing direct guidance for each group in separate specific documents.
- Overall, the strongest policies reflected a clear synergy between anti-bullying initiatives and other school initiatives.

Key Messages

- The first step towards promoting a whole school community approach to bullying prevention is to develop an anti-bullying policy.
- An anti-bullying policy provides a framework for how a school will tackle bullying.
- An anti-bullying policy provides the school community with clear expectations, direction, commitment and consistency in addressing all forms of bullying.

- An anti-bullying policy assists schools in moving beyond a crisis management approach to applying well-thought-out strategies of intervention at primary, secondary and tertiary level.

Notes

1. Farrington, D.P. and Ttofi, M.M., *School-Based Programmes to Reduce Bullying and Victimisation*, Campbell Systematic Reviews, Oslo: The Campbell Collaboration, 2009.
2. Varnava, G., *Towards a Non-Violent Society: Checkpoints for Schools*, London: National Children's Bureau, 2002.
3. Gittins, C. (ed.), *Violence Reduction in Schools – How to Make a Difference*, Strasbourg: Council of Europe, 2006.
4. Peter Galvin is the designer of the Leeds database and School Behaviour and Attendance Audit Instruments.
5. O'Moore, M., 'Preventing School Bullying: The Irish Experience' in Pepler, D. and Craig, W. (eds), *Understanding and Addressing Bullying: An International Experience*, Indiana: Author House, 2008.
6. Conducted by researchers in the Cardiff School of Social Sciences.

7 A TEACHER'S ROLE IN BULLYING PREVENTION

There is little doubt that teachers are critical in reducing bullying in schools. In spite of home circumstances, which may be causative of bullying and victimisation, schools nevertheless can make a significant difference.

A school environment causes children to feel upset and a failure when they are constantly being judged and graded in all that they do. If there are few opportunities to taste success, whether academically or in sport, children will have equally few opportunities to feel good about themselves. In such a competitive climate it would be surprising if emotions such as jealousy, envy and anger were not expressed. All too often these emotions find solace in putting others down.

While homes, too, can give rise to feelings of frustration, anger and poor self-worth, which can undoubtedly spill over into school, teachers are in an excellent position to counteract such emotions. They are also in a very strong position to counteract any poor role models that their students may encounter at home. They can achieve this by behaving in an exemplary manner in and out of class. By providing their students with positive and rewarding experiences they can make children feel good about themselves. They can also demonstrate that aggression or 'might makes right' (which may be played out in the home, on the screen or in the neighbourhood as a way of venting emotions) is unacceptable and makes for a poor member of society.

In Part One I mentioned that the root of aggressive behaviour can be in the home. Other factors that are strongly associated with aggression in school are poor morale among staff, inadequate supervision, a curriculum that affords too few opportunities of success and achievement and punishment that is too harsh and humiliating.

In effecting a whole school approach to bullying prevention, it is these factors that need to be given a high priority. My aim is, therefore, to address in more detail the steps that I believe teachers should take in order to achieve a reduction in the level of school bullying.

1. Create a School Ethos that is Positive and Friendly and Fosters a Culture of Respect

The school climate presents as one of the critical risk factors in bullying and violence. The aim should be, therefore, to create an ethos where all members of the school community can feel safe and work together in harmony. Teachers are very well placed to create a climate that is positive, welcoming, friendly and supportive. Indeed, the handbook written to support the Council of Europe's aim to prevent bullying and violence in schools have adopted the Spanish term *'convivencia'*, as it denotes the much desired climate of 'living together in harmony'.[1]

At the heart of a positive school climate is compassion, tolerance and respect of individual differences and diversity. There is no better way to promote such behaviour than having teachers model it on an everyday basis. It is critical that students should get no opportunity to interpret teacher interactions, whether with their colleagues or their students, as bullying behaviour. While teachers have the authority to direct and correct students when the occasion arises, care needs to be taken at all times that it is carried out in a manner that is not perceived as abusive, humiliating or as a putdown.

In their interactions with students, every opportunity should also be taken to promote equity and discourage prejudiced thinking and discrimination based on gender, race or disability. While it is beyond the scope of this book to discuss in any great detail the criteria that makes for high morale among teachers, it is widely accepted that happy and resourceful teachers make for happy and resourceful students. Thus, it is paramount that any issues there may be among staff that might mitigate against a climate of *convivencia* need to be addressed by the management of the school. Leaving situations to fester will only undermine a positive and friendly ethos, which is so critical to a successful whole school approach to bullying prevention.

2. Actively Discouraging Bullying Behaviour

I mentioned earlier in the book that students in Ireland perceive their teachers as intervening less often than their peers do when confronted with bullying behaviour. While the findings may have their roots in teachers not being as keenly aware as the students are of the bullying that takes place in school, the danger is that students are led to believe that teachers do not care that much about bullying, so why should they? To correct this perception, as well as promote the whole school approach to bullying, it is critical that teachers are observant and respond to all incidents that come to their attention. While it may not be opportune for them to address the incident on the spot if heading for a class or to some other scheduled activity, those involved should be alerted to the fact that note has been taken of their inappropriate behaviour and that it will be followed up. Firm sanctions, which include serious talks with the 'bullies', sending them to the principal, making them stay close to the teacher during break time and depriving them of privileges, have been shown to be very effective in reducing bullying, especially among younger children (under age eleven), whereas restorative approaches work best with children older than eleven. This is possibly due to their superior cognitive abilities and the ability to make rational decisions, as well as a decrease in impulsiveness.

In my view, it is critical that all incidents of bullying are addressed, no matter how trivial or minor they may appear, as this will reinforce the view that bullying is wrong and also that it is good to report it. Taking action will also reduce the risk of overlooking what might be an insidious 'drip, drip' campaign against a student, where each act on the face of it may appear insignificant. As we have seen, it is the relentless nature of the acts that is so damaging to those targeted. The recent case of Phoebe Prince, the Irish teenager who died by suicide in Massachusetts, should help to heighten the awareness of the need for teacher intervention. The reporting of the case[2] indicated that the authorities have criticised teachers and school staff who stood by while Phoebe (15) was subjected to persistent harassment. It is more than likely that sooner or later staff who ignore incidents of bullying will face charges of negligence.

In the Information Box on p. 144 I have listed the behaviours that I believe should guide teachers when dealing with incidents of bullying.

3. Challenging All Single Acts of Inappropriate Aggression

In recognising that bullying is a process where a single act of aggression may be the precursor to bullying, I believe it is important that all acts of inappropriate aggression are challenged. In that way there is a chance to prevent the escalation of aggression that is so characteristic of bullying. It also reinforces the view that inappropriate aggression, even on a once-off basis, is an unacceptable way to handle disagreements or pent-up emotions.

From the investigation conducted by the United States Secret Service and the United States Department of Education into school shootings, for example, we learn that many of the attackers felt bullied, persecuted or injured prior to the violent attack. In one situation, for instance, they reported that one of the attackers was described by fellow students as the kid that everyone teased. In witness statements from the incident, fellow students described how virtually every student had at some point thrown the attacker against a locker, tripped him in the hall, held his head under water in a pool or thrown things at him. Noteworthy also is that several schoolmates had noticed that the attacker acted differently in the days preceding the attack, in that he seemed more annoyed by and less tolerant of the teasing than usual.[3]

One can't help thinking how different the situation might have been had each individual act been challenged. Not only would it have provided opportunities to correct the inappropriate aggression on the part of the offending students, but it might also have unearthed the fact that the individual acts were symptomatic of a campaign of bullying.

There is little doubt that teachers have every opportunity to model and teach constructive ways of dealing with negative incidents. Every negative act should be seen as an opportunity for learning. Indeed, it was the 'broken window' policing philosophy where all minor offences were dealt with on a consistent basis that helped New York to turn its seemingly hopeless crime situation around to one that became a model for the rest of the world. Similarly 'Gran Skole' in Oslo, Norway, can boast a similar success story.[4]

4. Promoting a Culture of Disclosure to Break the Code of Silence

It is not uncommon for the viewpoint to exist that telling a member of staff that another student is being bullied violates the unwritten but powerful 'code of silence'. A code of silence has the potential to not only deny victims the opportunity to have the bullying stopped, but it also prevents corrective action to be taken against the aggressors and, most importantly, the causes of the bullying behaviour to be addressed.

Schools should, therefore, do all in their power to challenge the 'code of silence' and promote instead a culture of disclosure. Students should be taught to associate the reporting of threats of injury, bullying and violence with positive attributes such as good moral courage and strength. Standing by, saying and doing nothing should be regarded as a sign of weakness. There should be nothing honourable about being in possession of information that is damaging to another person's mental and physical health. Reporting incidents of bullying is not telling tales but behaving responsibly. If we could socially engineer our students to adopt such attitudes we would see a rapid reduction in the level of bullying, because not only would it empower victims to come forward, it would undoubtedly also motivate those inclined to bully to think twice before launching an attack. No longer would the dice be loaded in their favour with the victim or the bystanders keeping quiet.

5. Developing and Maintaining a Classroom Environment that is Positive, Co-operative and Rewarding

There is no running away from the fact that with students spending most of their day confined to their classrooms in a sedentary manner, there is likely to be a build-up of emotions. These emotions can as easily be fuelled as they can be calmed, depending on the atmosphere that is generated by the classroom teacher. Ill feelings, for example, which can arise so easily as a result of negative teacher interactions, will be either internalised (unease, anxiety, withdrawal) or externalised (aggressive or coercive behaviour and bullying).

To achieve a much desired positive and bully-free atmosphere in the classroom means preventing emotions from running high, especially frustration and anger. Teachers can do this by taking a leaf out of Maslow's book.[5] This means that at all times they should do all in their power to avoid threatening the basic needs of their students, these being:

- Physiological needs (hunger, thirst, temperature in room)
- Safety needs (freedom from threat)
- Belongingness (friendship)
- Esteem needs (recognition, achievement).

I believe that the best way to meet the individual learning and emotional needs of students is for teachers to adopt a teaching style that makes use of co-operative learning structures.[6] These mean that students work together in small groups of four or five to achieve a common goal. Groups should contain students of mixed ability and, if in co-educational schools, there should be a mix of boys and girls. If possible, different ethnic and social classes should also be represented. The principles of effective co-operative learning groups are as follows:

- The group rather than the individual earns the reward
- All members of the group must contribute
- All members of the group must have an equal opportunity to contribute
- Each student is expected to improve on previous performance
- Competition between teams is acceptable.

Co-operative learning draws on the psychology of team sports. It is like bringing the sports arena into the classroom. Each member of the team does his or her utmost to have their team win, so it is not like the more traditional group work which ran the risk of one or two students doing all the work while everyone got the credit. Instead, with the co-operative learning structures the success of the group depends on building:

- **positive interdependence:** the success of the group depends on the success of each member;

109

- **individual accountability:** each student is responsible for learning the material;
- **social skills:** the interpersonal and communication skills that are necessary for effective group interaction.

Teachers have found that by integrating the elements of co-operative learning structures into their lessons, the students are more motivated to learn and it leads to higher achievements. It also increases their self-esteem and helps to increase acceptance and respect for other students. Indeed, the *Facilitators' Manual on Cooperative Learning*, produced by the Association for Supervision and Curriculum Development (ASCD), reports that many teachers found that co-operative learning 'revitalised their classrooms, rekindling the joy of learning and the joy of teaching'.[7]

It should be pointed out, however, that co-operative learning is not something that can be learned successfully overnight. It requires time to refine the techniques and students need time to develop the co-operative skills that make group work most effective (see Recommended Reading). Courses are also available that link in with Trinity College's School of Education Diploma in Co-operative Learning and their Masters in Education programme.

Reward Structures

If the introduction of co-operative learning structures is not an option in the immediate future, there is nonetheless considerable scope to change the atmosphere in the classroom by manipulating the different reward structures that may be used on an everyday basis. There are four main types:

- **Individual competition:** only a few students can obtain the rewards at the expense of their classmates. Grading according to a predetermined number of A, B, C, D and F grades is an example of this structure.
- **Group competition:** groups of students co-operate among themselves to compete with other groups for limited rewards.
- **Individual reward:** students work independently to achieve a learning outcome attributing success or failure to their own personal effort.

- **Group reward:** rewards are given solely on the basis of the quality of a group's performance. The focus is on shared effort and mutual obligation as the basis for motivation and each member in the group receives the same reward.

Achieving a good balance between these reward structures will create a learning environment in which students should feel comfortable and secure. A student who feels secure will more readily attend to the learning task at hand, while a threatened student will have greater difficulty concentrating on learning and may instead expend their energies protecting their self-esteem from the threat of failure. Students who are under pressure to protect their self-esteem will tend to use any of the following all too familiar strategies:

- Making little or no effort in order to avoid humiliation and rejection, reasoning with themselves that with no effort there can be no failure and with no failure there can be no humiliation.
- Becoming a perfectionist and easily upset at the prospect of failure. Too many hours are therefore spent on work in order to eliminate any risk of failure.
- Behaving in a boastful, aggressive and bullying manner. The 'I could if I tried' or 'I haven't tried yet' mentality is common. Students displaying this form of compensatory behaviour might be expected to target their more successful classmates or those with special needs, as putting them down makes them feel good.

In view of the negative impact of competitive reward structures in the classroom, it is recommended that they are used sparingly. Indeed, it has been suggested that co-operative reward structures should be used 60 to 70 per cent of the time, with individualistic reward structure being used 20 per cent of the time and competitive reward structure 10 to 20 per cent of the time.

Promoting Restorative Approaches to Dealing with Bullying

A restorative approach to dealing with wrongdoing is a relatively new way of thinking about actions deserving of correction or punishment. It has its roots in restorative justice, where the underlying values are based on respect for the dignity of all involved in and affected by the crime. Priority is given to addressing the needs of all those involved and to empower them to communicate their thoughts and feelings in an open and honest way.

Restorative justice was recommended as having considerable value as a means of dealing with bullying and violence. It should, therefore, form part of a whole school approach to bullying prevention.[8] The goal in choosing a restorative approach for dealing with bullying would be to build understanding, encourage accountability and provide an opportunity for healing. The approach aims to encourage aggressors to:

- take responsibility for their hurtful behaviour in a meaningful way;
- gain insight into the causes and effects of that behaviour on others;
- change their negative/anti-social behaviour.

The restorative approach most importantly also gives the targeted person or victim the opportunity to state the impact of the bullying and to ask questions, receive answers and gain an understanding of why they were targeted. The process also allows for the victim to receive an apology or some other form of amends, which can help to bring closure to the victimisation.

Rather than fuelling resentment and reprisals, which so often characterises punitive approaches, promoting a restorative approach to indiscipline and bullying reinforces instead the values that make for a non-violent school community. The values that underpin restorative justice are as follows:

- Mutual respect
- Acknowledgement
- Openness
- Patience
- Sensitivity
- Empathy
- Empowerment
- Connectedness
- Accountability

- Encouragement
- Sharing ideas
- Importance of feelings, needs and rights
- Willingness to listen to each other.

In Chapter 11 I will list details on specific methods that are restorative in nature, which can be used by school staff in dealing with aggression, bullying and violence.

Using the Curriculum

The curriculum can be used to tackle issues associated with bullying, both traditional and cyber. It can heighten students' awareness of bullying and the school's anti-bullying policy. It can also help students learn to become more aware of their emotions and understand the reasons for them. They can also learn to express their feelings and attitudes more openly and constructively. This should then equip them to behave in a more pro-social manner and to deal with conflicts, prejudice and discrimination in a more constructive manner in and out of school.

I am of the strong belief that there is no school subject that does not lend itself to promoting an anti-bullying ethos. While English and art may have the upper hand, subjects such as history, geography and even mathematics can also provide excellent arenas for raising awareness. Geography and history, for example, offer up valuable opportunities to discuss the negative aspects of power by making references to colonisation and exploitation, and to the long line of dictators throughout history. In mathematics, students can apply statistical methods to data collected from a class or school survey on bullying. Physical education and sports also provide excellent opportunities for promoting co-operation and for learning to control aggression and violence. For further examples, see *Dealing with Bullying in Schools*.[9]

Visual Material

Videos, DVDs, films and virtual reality games, such as in the Finnish Kiva anti-bullying programme, are also extremely effective in illustrating bullying and promoting discussions on why students bully each other, what the effects of bullying are on the victims, bullies and bystanders, and what students can do to both prevent and stop bullying.

The nationally-produced DVD, *Silent Witnesses*, depicting post-primary students in Ireland, is a powerful tool for stimulating discussion. It is particularly apt as it touches on characteristics that underpin the tragic cases of Leanne Wolfe and Phoebe Prince, characteristics which Brenda Power, in her article 'Money and Power: the Reasons Why School Bullies Get Free Rein', describes so well.[10]

Beat Bullying provides good short educational videos for stimulating debate and discussion on cyber-bullying. There are also valuable visual resources to be found in the individual chapters on working with children and young people and with parents.

Drama

Drama may be used to great effect either by having students develop and perform their own or other playwrights' plays, but also if necessary bringing in theatre-in-education groups.

There may be readers who, for example, remember the very successful performances in both primary (launched in 1994) and post-primary schools (launched in 1996) by Paula Greevy, Producer/Director of Sticks and Stones Theatre Company. Once the performances were over, each class group that had watched the performance met with one of the actors for a question and answer session. The performances were to act as a catalyst for further exercises to raise awareness by the class teachers and to form part of the process of developing an anti-bullying policy in the schools, as recommended by the Department of Education's guidelines at the time. The handbooks for teachers that accompanied the performances still stand well today, with valuable information for teachers as to how to prevent and deal with bullying behaviour.

Other Mediums

Whatever medium is used to promote awareness of bullying, the key points to get across when talking to students of all ages and abilities about bullying behaviour are summed up in the Information Box on p. 100. I have also included questions (see Information Box below) that can be used to facilitate a discussion with students. If they are made aware that their viewpoints will be given consideration and acted upon, the exercise should prove to be very stimulating.

Information Box: Questions for Discussion with Students

1. How can we make our school a safer place?
2. How can we stop bullying:
   - In the playground?
   - In the classroom?
   - In the corridors and toilets?
   - At lunch times and break times?
   - Outside school?
3. How can we make it easier for students to tell an adult if they are being bullied?
4. What should teachers and other adults do if someone is being bullied:
   - To help the bullied students?
   - To help the bullying students?
5. What can you and other students do about bullying?

It should be noted that when raising awareness in classes in which there are children with special needs, care will have to be taken that the level of presentation is appropriate to their individual needs.

Cyber-Bullying

The fact that nearly 20 per cent of teenagers have had the person who was cyber-bullying them pretend to be someone else in order to trick them and get them to reveal personal information[11] indicates that learning about cyber-safety cannot be left to chance. Fortunately, there is evidence to show that education strategies are of significant benefit when delivered by teachers. For example, a review of existing Australian and international cyber-safety research reports that 80 per cent of pupils who were shown a documentary video which addresses cyber-safety changed their online behaviour. There was a significant decrease in the number of students who would share personal details with someone they met online only.[12]

While there is no specific anti-bullying curriculum designed as yet for Irish schools, an internet safety teaching and learning programme for post-primary schools has been developed.[13] The programme consists of a teachers' internet safety lesson and resource pack for first- to third-year Junior Certificate SPHE classes. The resources facilitate discussion on:

- students' safety issues when using the internet;
- the opportunities and benefits of surfing the net and being online;
- the responsible use of networking sites;
- procedures for protecting personal safety and security when online;
- students' awareness of the potential risks in disclosing personal information online and posting inappropriate photographic material.

The thirteen lessons in the programme contain teacher notes, glossary of key terminology, lesson plans, activity sheets and downloadable resources.[14] For further details on resources that can be used to heighten students' awareness of cyber-safety and cyber-bullying, see Cyber Training (www.cybertraining-project.org), a European Commission project to help teachers and the school-going population to keep safe while cyber communicating. Also of value is the most recent EU Kids Online report, launched on 21 October 2010.[15] An EU Kids Online Irish national report will be published in Februrary 2011.

It should be noted that the key messages for students tend to be the same irrespective of which website issues advice. In the Information Box below, I have listed the advice that I feel is most pertinent for students to heed.

Information Box: Key Messages for Cyber-Safety and Countering Cyber-Bullying

- Be cautious about disclosing personal information.
- Treat your password as you would your toothbrush.
- Give your mobile number or email address to only those you trust.
- Posting messages on the internet can be seen instantly and by large audiences.
- Electronic communications can be held indefinitely as a record.
- Think of the consequences before you send a message.
- Treat others online as you would like to be treated yourself, i.e. with respect.
- Don't reply to abusive messages.
- Keep abusive messages as evidence.
- Block the sender.
- Tell a trusted friend, cyber-mentor, teacher or parent.
- Report serious issues to an adult or directly to the website or mobile phone service provider.
- If the cyber attacks are persistent and threatening to your mental and physical health, get in touch with the Gardaí. It is illegal (in Ireland) to send or post messages to another person that are knowingly false, grossly offensive, indecent, obscene or menacing for the purpose of causing annoyance or anxiety.

Improving Playground Supervision

As much bullying takes place in the playground due to boredom, overcrowding and out-of-sight areas, schools would be well advised to look for strategies that can help to prevent and decrease bullying behaviour in the playground. The strategies, many of which are low cost, include the following:

- Improving the environmental quality and educational use of the playground to allow for educational, social, physical and creative activities (see the UK anti-bullying pack for schools, *Bullying: Don't Suffer in Silence* for ideas).[16]
- Increase playground supervision. If the budget allows, recruit specially trained supervisors or set up a rota for the students themselves to assist in supervision.
- Supervisors should wear some high visibility clothing as is done in Norway's Zero[17] anti-bullying programme and in Finland's Kiva anti-bulling programme.[18]
- Train all who supervise to distinguish between horseplay/play-fighting and inappropriate physical fighting and bullying. Also look out for marginalised and isolated students.
- Have an incident book to record all serious incidents and apply the school's sanctions when there is a breach in the code of playground behaviour.

Key Messages

- Teachers hold the key to reducing the level of bullying in schools.
- Teachers can make a whole school approach to bullying work by:
  o creating and reinforcing a positive and friendly ethos in the school;
  o promoting a culture of respect and dignity;
  o discouraging all bullying behaviour that comes to their attention;
  o challenging all single acts of inappropriate aggression;
  o promoting a culture of disclosure;
  o empowering bystanders to take action;
  o developing a classroom climate that is positive and rewarding to the students, using whenever possible co-operative learning structures;
  o promoting restorative approaches to dealing with indiscipline and bullying;

o using the curriculum and visual material to heighten awareness of the cost of bullying to individuals, the school community and the wider society;

o improving the playground environment and supervision.

Notes

1. Council of Europe, *Violence Reduction in Schools: How to Make a Difference*, Council of Europe Publishing, 2006.
2. *Evening Herald,* 30 March 2010.
3. Yossekuil, B., Fein, R., Reddy, M., Borum, R. and Modzeleski, W., *The Final Report and the Findings of the Safe School Initiative: Implications for the Prevention of School Attacks in the United States*, US Department of Education, Office of Elementary and Secondary Education, Safe and Drug-Free Schools Program and US Secret Service National Threat Assessment Centre, Washington, DC, 2002.
4. O'Moore, M. and Minton, S.J., *Tackling Violence in Schools in Norway: A Broad Approach*, an evaluation report: http://.old.gold.ac.uk/connect/evaluationnorway.html.
5. Maslow, A.H., *Motivation and Personality*, 3rd Edition, New York: Harper Row, 1987.
6. Pioneered and developed by Robert Slavin and brothers David Johnson and Roger Johnson.
7. Slavin, R.E., *Cooperative Learning: Theory, Research and Practice*, 2nd Edition, Massachusetts: Allyn & Bacon, 1995.
8. I had the good fortune to learn about restorative justice from Dobrinka Chankova, a Bulgarian lawyer who was a partner in the European project VISTA, which developed an online course for trainers of the whole school approach to bullying (www.vista.org.uk). The materials that made up the VISTA course, inclusive of that pertaining to restorative justice, were later adapted as part of another European project (VISTOP) to provide self-directed courses for policymakers, teachers and parents. Any reader wishing to learn more about restorative justice can access the materials by logging on to www.vistop.org/ebook.
9. O'Moore, M. and Minton, S.J., *Dealing With Bullying in Schools: A Training Manual for Teachers, Parents and Other Professionals*, London: Paul Chapman, 2004, pp. 40–46.
10. *Sunday Times*, 4 April 2010.
11. The US National Crime Prevention Council, 2008: www.ncpc.org/cyberbullying.
12. Dooley, J.S., Cross, D., Hearn, L. and Treyvaud, R., *Review of Existing Australian and International Cyber-Safety Research*, Edith Cowan University, Commonwealth of Australia: Child Health Promotion Research Centre, 2009.
13. Created by The National Council for Technology in Education's Internet Safety initiative, in collaboration with the Department of Education and Skill's SPHE Support Service: www.webwise.ie. Under 'Learning Resources'.
14. http://www.webwise.ie/article.aspx?id=8664.
15. Livingstone, S. and Haddon, L., *EU Kids Online: Final Report 2010*, London School of Economics (eukidsonline@lse.ac.uk).

16. *Bullying – Don't Suffer in Silence*, an anti-bullying pack for schools, UK Department for Education and Skills, 2006.

17. Zero anti-bullying programme: www.skole.karmoy.kommune.no/zero/zero_englishleaflet.pdf.

18. Kiva anti-bullying programme: http://www.kivakoulu.fi.

8 PROMOTING POSITIVE SELF-ESTEEM

Earlier in the book I said that Irish children and adolescents who bullied had significantly lower self-esteem than their peers who did not bully. The fact that they had lower self-esteem suggests that they did not feel good enough about themselves (globally or in some domain) to avoid having to compensate for feelings of inadequacy. Why, otherwise, did they proactively or reactively need to empower themselves by putting others down? From our results, it would appear that the more often children and teens bully their peers, the lower their self-esteem.[1]

I believe that teachers are in the best position to help parents build the self-esteem that children and adolescents need to meet the challenges of life, both inside and outside of school. With good self-esteem comes a sense of emotional well-being and a desire for new learning. Raising students' self-esteem will result in:

- reduced anxiety;
- increased assertiveness;
- reduced aggression;
- improved relationships;
- increased confidence;
- increased willingness to try things out and to learn from mistakes;
- reduced disruption.

The added value beyond good social and emotional adjustment of good self-esteem has been shown by Emer Symth (1999) in her book, *Do Schools Differ?*[2] She found that students, especially those with high academic self-esteem, tended to achieve higher than average grades in school. However, it is equally recognised that the positive relationship that exists between self-esteem and achievement does not necessarily imply that high self-esteem causes high grades. Instead there is evidence to suggest that high self-esteem develops from:

- achieving an acceptable level of competence in school;
- valuing academic success;
- being given support and positive feedback for one's efforts and achievements.

For these reasons the role that teachers can play in developing a sturdy self-esteem cannot be underestimated.

Many students believe that ability is fixed (reinforced by rigid streaming in schools) and that, therefore, putting effort into cognitive or scholastic pursuits is a waste of effort. The students who feel this way tend to be those who are low on self-efficacy as a result of negative teaching and learning experiences. Any success that they may have will be attributed to luck or an easy task. This contrasts with their peers who have high levels of self-esteem, who will attribute success to effort and ability, and failure to lack of effort.

To overcome a defeatist attitude to learning and achievement, which so often gives way to apathy, withdrawal or disruptive and bullying behaviour, will require a change of attitude. However, this will only come about if teachers themselves believe that intelligence is a developmental process and not something that is fixed from birth. Fortunately, there is now increasing evidence to show that when teachers believe in their students' capabilities they will see improvements in their motivation to learn and their achievements. The resulting gain on the students' levels of confidence and self-efficacy will further strengthen their motivational orientation and scope to achieve, which in turn will help to maintain good levels of self-esteem.

With the interdependence of self-esteem, motivation and achievement it is clear why we have such well-worn sayings as 'success breeds success' or 'practice makes perfect'. However, the challenge for teachers is how to win students around to believing that these sayings are true and how critical it is that ability is not fixed but is dependent on effort.

Tips to Promoting a Positive Self-Concept in Students

Reward effort. For students of all ages to appreciate that they have value and can learn requires that they are provided with experiences that will demonstrate to them that success is not attributed to ability alone, but that it responds to sustained and persistent effort. Teachers need to reward effort as well as success.

While it may be difficult to determine the level of effort that any one student puts into a piece of work, it can be judged by comparing it to other work that the student has carried out. The standard of work is likely to reflect the amount of effort put in. By splitting the marks to be awarded for effort and presentation on the one hand, and content and standard of work on the other, it should allow for effort to be rewarded. So even if the content and standard is not great, the positive recognition or praise that is awarded for the effort will motivate the student to work harder. By trying harder, content and standard will undoubtedly improve and so the end result will be achieved: that of showing the student that ability is not fixed and effort pays dividends for achievement and self-worth.

Care should also be taken to communicate encouraging results in performance and behaviour to parents. This allows parents to take pride in their child, which in turn will help them as parents to foster a positive attitude to schoolwork and academic achievement and, indeed, good behaviour, rather than the often counterproductive defensive, rejecting and alienating stance that so often results from conveying negative reports to parents.

A most recent example of the value of rewarding effort and paying attention to the individual strengths of students and communicating these results to parents is that of Wellington College in the UK. In the article 'Teaching an Old School New Tricks'[3] we learn how Anthony Sheldon, on his appointment to the college as headmaster, achieved remarkable results for his pupils by focusing on and rewarding effort and, most importantly, playing to the students' strengths (what they enjoy and are good at) rather than their weaknesses. Students who earlier would have been regarded as average were now achieving results that would usually characterise the more high-achieving students. Quintessentially, he took the students' sense of happiness and well-being to the heart of education, creating a positive school climate with the result that he achieved optimal results for his students. He also not surprisingly gained huge support from parents who saw their sons and daughters make significant gains in their learning and level of happiness. Needless to say, disruption and bullying behaviour was significantly reduced.

Use praise. Few adults will deny the pleasure associated with being praised. Many purr like a kitten when praised and so it is with children and adolescents. There is, however, a growing view that praise may be damaging in that it can give a false sense of self-worth. This is the case when it is used indiscriminately without any regard to the effort expended or the meaning of the accomplishment, for example, whether the task was easy or difficult for the student to perform and succeed in. Otherwise, in educational psychology circles, when praise is used contingent on appropriate performance and behaviour, or approximations to appropriate performance and behaviour, it is seen as a powerful motivational technique. It increases achievement, motivation, academic performance and behaviour, all of which, as I have noted, are dependent on each other in promoting and maintaining good self-esteem. It should be noted that introverts have been found to be more responsive to praise than have extroverts. A reason put forward for this finding is that introverts are more interested in their own feelings and thoughts, whereas extroverts are more caught up with events outside of themselves.

Gage and Berliner, in their book on Educational Psychology,[4] provide useful guidelines for teachers for the effective and ineffective use of praise. For fear that their guidelines may not be sourced and in recognition of the extraordinary value of praise, I list in the Information Box below what I believe to be the most important aspects to consider when using praise.

Information Box: Effective Praise
1. It is given contingent on some tangible outcome.
2. It mentions the specifics of what has been accomplished.
3. It demonstrates a spontaneous and varied response to the student's achievement.
4. It rewards the attainment of some standard of performance that includes effort.
5. It includes feedback on the competence or value of the work.

6. It draws attention to the student's own task-related behaviour and thinking about problem-solving.
7. It draws attention to and builds on earlier efforts and accomplishments.
8. It recognises the significant effort or success of work that is difficult for the student.
9. It attributes success to effort and ability, implying that similar success can be expected again.

Apply the Ten-Step Model of Jack Canfield

There is no shortage of material, whether in books or educational packs, that is devoted to promoting strategies to enhance self-esteem. However, over the years I have recommended to my students the model developed by Jack Canfield (1990), one of the past presidents of self-esteem seminars in the USA, because of the ease with which I believe the steps can be worked into every lesson and into any dealings that may be had with students on an individual basis. The steps are as follows.

1. Assume an attitude of 100 per cent responsibility. Introduce students to the formula E (events) + R (their response to the events) = O (outcomes). Grasping this principle encourages them to not blame others for negative outcomes, but rather take responsibility for changing their responses. With this approach students learn to understand that they have choices and that it is their choice that determines the consequence for which they must take responsibility. This principle also feeds into assertive discipline, a strategy which I will detail later when dealing specifically with curbing inappropriate behaviour, as it helps to build self-discipline. An example that Canfield gives is: 'Hit someone who yells at you, and you go to the principal's office. Respond with humour or by ignoring the person and you stay out of trouble.'[5]

2. Focus on the positive. In order to feel successful you have to experience success. Many students may feel that they have never experienced success, because they equate success with something tangible, such as receiving a school award or a sporting medal. However, by encouraging students to recall an earlier stage in their lives, they will often uncover aspects that can give them cause to feel proud and successful. In recognising past achievements, the stage is set for 'if you could do it then, you can do it now'.

124

Focusing on the positive finds support in Seligman's School of Positive Psychology, which very much follows in the footsteps of Humanistic Psychologists such as Maslow, whom I made reference to earlier. Essentially, we should all forget what we are not good at and get on with what we are good at. The release of positive emotions that flow from students when having positive or successful experiences not only boosts their determination to succeed, but also benefits their interpersonal relationships as the negative emotions of stress, anxiety and anger, which are commonly associated with failure and unhappiness, have no recourse.

3. *Learn to monitor self-talk.* There is no counting the number of thoughts each of us has each day, although a figure of 12,000 has been put forward for an average person and 50,000 for a deep thinker. As many of the thoughts are about ourselves, the most important thing is to think positively because they will be the blueprints for our actions. Thoughts such as 'I'm hopeless at maths' can be replaced, for example, with 'I need to give it more time'. If faced with derogatory remarks about their looks, negative thoughts can be replaced with 'beauty is in the eye of the beholder; I'm smart and I accept myself the way I am'.

The message to give students is to say 'cancel, cancel' whenever they hear themselves or others say something negative about them. They should then quickly replace the negative with a positive. This is the essence of the 'fogging' technique, which is very effective for students who are bullied. For example, when abuse is hurled at them they can cancel it out by visualising themselves taking cover in a fog and, in addition, saying to themselves, 'No matter what you say or do to me I am a worthwhile person'. Having a mantra such as this is a powerful antidote to all negative thoughts and statements that get implanted into one's thinking.

4. *Use support groups in the classroom.* It is not uncommon for students to leave the classroom each day feeling unhappy and discouraged due to lack of recognition. As a means to overcome feelings of alienation, each day, if necessary, students can be paired off or placed in small groups (these being different on each occasion) where they spend a few minutes in class time talking to each other about specific topics, for example, 'What record would you break if you could break any

125

record in the world?' or, 'Which charity would you give money to if you won the lotto and why that charity?' Such activities facilitate positive experiences with everyone having a voice. Also, by sharing feelings, thoughts and behaviours with their classmates, positive relationships are fostered.

5. *Identify strengths and resources.* Critical in helping students to expand their self-esteem is for them to achieve a broadened awareness of their strengths and resources. To help with this, Canfield advises teachers to have students in their support groups write down and tell each other what they see as their positive qualities and strengths. As their assessments need to be realistic as well as positive, teachers should note the areas that need development in order to help students value themselves more so that they can reach their goals.

6. *Clarify your vision.* With a clear vision comes motivation. Questions that can help students to clarify their visions are: 'If you won a sports scholarship to a university, what would you choose to study?' or, 'If you were granted three wishes, what would you wish for?' Sharing their visions, which are non-threatening and fun, with the class not only helps students become more aware of themselves, their desires, their ambitions and, above all, their uniqueness, it also provides opportunities to see commonalities with other students, which can be a catalyst to forming new positive relationships with peers.

7. *Set goals and objectives.* Have students set short-term goals. This is a well-established technique and has the effect of significantly enhancing learning, motivation and a sense of mastery when applied to academic subjects. The intrinsic interest and self-efficacy that develops from meeting goals successfully helps to build a positive self-concept. Canfield helps students to not only set goals and objectives for themselves, but also for their family, school and community.

8. *Use visualisation.* The power of visualisation is increasingly being recognised as a powerful tool and is used to great effect in sports and in holistic or alternative medicine. Essentially, students can be encouraged, as sportsmen are trained to, to visualise themselves achieving their desired goal, for example, sitting an exam and passing it. Having students spend, as Canfield does, five minutes per day visualising each of their goals and objectives as if they were already

achieved is extremely energising, releasing creativity and motivation, with the result that it can produce radical results very quickly.

9. Take action. The message that should be emphasised to students is that to be successful they have to 'do the doing'. The example that Canfield gives to his students is, 'You cannot hire someone else to do your push-ups for you and expect to develop your muscles'. The best a teacher can do for their students is, therefore, stretch them into more and more action steps, doing things they previously did not think they were capable of.

10. Respond to feedback and persevere. We have all heard the idioms, 'Perseverance is the name of the game' and, 'If at first you don't succeed, try and try again'. However, providing living examples of the phenomenon is more effective than drumming in age-old sayings. It is inspirational for students to hear stories of individuals – local, national or international – who, against all odds, have achieved some ambition of theirs. For example, recently we heard of an Australian teenage girl, Jessica Watson, who sailed around the world in her ten-metre yacht called Ella's Pink Lady. When hailed as a hero for her record-breaking sail, she responded: 'I don't consider myself a hero, I'm an ordinary girl. You don't have to be someone special to achieve something amazing, you've just got to have a dream, believe in it and work hard. I'd like to think I've proved that anything really is possible if you set your mind to it.'[6]

Another valuable thing also practised by Canfield is to teach students to use mistakes for growth, to use positive as well as negative feedback to their advantage and to persevere until they accomplish their goals.

If Canfield's ten steps are used by classroom teachers to form part of a whole school approach to bullying prevention, the gains to be achieved are many. Raising the students' confidence, self-esteem and achievements will go a long way to establishing a positive and supportive classroom climate, thereby removing the need for compensatory behaviour such as aggression, bullying and violence.

It is to be noted that Canfield has more recently developed a ten-step model built on the same principles as above that adults can use to help them reach peak performance and organisational success.[7]

Key Messages

- There is a strong relationship between bullying and self-esteem. Students who bully and are bullied have lower self-esteem than children who are not involved in bullying.
- Children with a sturdy sense of self-experience tend to experience emotional well-being and academic success.
- Success breeds success, so give students positive learning experiences to promote a positive self-concept.
- Reward effort and use praise contingent on some tangible outcome.
- At all times promote positive self-esteem by adopting or adapting Canfield's ten-step model of self-esteem.

Notes

1. O'Moore, M. and Kirkham, C., 'Self-Esteem and its Relationship to Bullying Behaviour' in *Aggressive Behaviour*, 27 (2001), pp. 269–283.
2. Smyth, E., *Do Schools Differ? Academic and Personal Development Among Pupils in the Second-Level Sector*, Dublin: Oak Tree Press & Economic and Social Research Institute, 1999.
3. Wood, R., 'Teaching an Old School New Tricks', *Sunday Times Magazine*, 13 December 2009, pp. 33–42.
4. Gage, N.L. and Berliner, D.C., *Educational Psychology*, 6th Edition, New York: Houghton Mifflin, 1998.
5. Canfield, J., 'Improving Students' Self-Esteem' in *Education Leadership*, 48 (1990), pp. 48–50.
6. *Irish Times*, 17 May 2010.
7. www.jackcanfield.com.

9

PROMOTING EFFECTIVE CLASSROOM DISCIPLINE

You may recall that the study referred to earlier in Chapter 6 of the effectiveness of programmes worldwide to reduce bullying found that the following elements were among the most effective:

- Disciplinary methods
- Classroom rules
- Classroom management.

No effort to prevent and counter bullying can be complete without paying attention to these crucial components.

In recent times there has been a groundswell of concern about student behaviour, especially from the teacher unions. Media reports have also abounded of disaffected, disinterested, disruptive and increasingly violent pupils.[1]

Generally speaking, there is no smoke without a fire, so the mounting concern surrounding student misbehaviour prompted a Task Force report on student behaviour in second-level schools.[2] It is to the report's credit that it gives full recognition to the fact that disruptive behaviour, including bullying, takes a significant toll on the school community. Students, for example, cannot achieve optimal learning when there are unacceptable levels of noise, rowdiness or verbal or physical aggression in the classroom. Teachers suffer too and, as the report states, disruptive behaviour is a 'source of ongoing stress, disillusionment and loss of morale'. Indeed, Sean Flynn, the educational correspondent for the *Irish Times*, reports: '80 per cent of teachers say discipline and other issues are increasing, distracting from the core business of teaching and learning.'[3]

Schools must, therefore, take responsibility for socialising students so that they behave in acceptable ways. Pamela Munn, the author of *Promoting Positive Discipline*, a project funded by the Scottish Office, is of the opinion, for example, that good discipline is an end in itself. She states: 'Socialising pupils to behave in acceptable ways is an inescapable part of a school's job, instilling in pupils values such as honesty, respect and diligence. So when we hear of violence in schools and classrooms we are concerned for the well-being of our society, for social cohesion.'[4]

To correct the growing concern around student misbehaviour, the Task Force recommended that a systematic approach be taken, which must focus on:

- the school ethos;
- relationship-building across the school community;
- the quality of teaching and learning;
- school leadership;
- classroom management skills of the teaching staff;
- the suitability of the curriculum;
- level of parental support;
- the efficacy of the school's attempt to be proactive in minimising disruption.

Readers will recognise that all of these elements echo those which make up a whole school community approach to bullying prevention. Although bullying behaviour is not synonymous with disruptive behaviour, where there is growth in disruption there tends to be a corresponding growth in bullying. It has been shown that disruptive children are often anti-social, exhibiting aggression towards other children and staff through bullying, refusal to co-operate, disobedience, stealing, lying and tantrums.

It is paramount, therefore, that teachers find effective means to promote good behaviour in their classrooms. When students' needs are met in the classroom and they feel respected, there will be less cause for them to take their frustrations out on others, either within the classroom or outside of it.

Teachers often use punitive responses as sanctions, but punitive and reactive responses can provoke an increase in unacceptable behaviour, with students reacting to the authoritarian climate with more aggression and rule-breaking in the face of punishment. Indeed, the European partners with whom I worked to develop VISTA,[5] an online training manual for dealing with violence in school, all agreed that the use of punitive responses does not produce more control and order in the classroom, since it increases the difference in power between the teacher and the students. In fact, we recognised that the large differentiation, which provokes the authoritarian climate, stands to increase conflicts between teacher and pupils.

From my experience of classroom teaching and supervision, I believe there is no better way to achieve effective classroom discipline than to adopt assertive discipline. This is a technique developed by Lee Canter and provides teachers with a structure for managing their classrooms in a way that will allow them to accomplish their academic goals, while at the same time teaching their students self-discipline. Canter recognises that the principles on which effective classroom management is based are as follows:

- Students need to know their teachers' behavioural expectations
- Students need to be taught responsible behaviour
- Students need limits
- Students need positive recognition and support.

Canter and Canter[6] contend that the assertive teacher 'must be willing and able to set consistent, positive behaviour limits while providing warmth and support to students for their appropriate behaviour'. Teachers are reminded that conditions in society and in home environments that lack support leave many students with only their teacher to look to as a role model for caring, as well as disciplined and socially-acceptable behaviour. The beauty of assertive discipline is that it is not at odds with what students themselves believe teachers need to do in order to eliminate the bullying and violence of students and staff. For example, students are very clear that teachers need to:

- set clear limits and standards;
- take consistent action if regulations are violent;
- give pupils a positive signal when they display pro-social behaviour;
- give pupils a warning before punishing anti-social behaviour;
- act consistently and treat pupils fairly;
- listen actively to pupils, taking their opinions seriously.

Assertive Discipline: The Steps

The first step is to develop a discipline plan. A classroom discipline plan provides the structure that will enable teachers to clarify the behaviours they want from their students and what they in turn can expect from their teachers. Importantly, a classroom discipline plan stresses supportive feedback as the most powerful tool at a teacher's disposal for encouraging responsible behaviour and for raising self-esteem. The plan consists of three parts:

- Rules that students must follow at all times
- Supportive feedback that students will receive consistently for obeying the rules
- Corrective action that teachers will use consistently when there is a breach of the rules.

In keeping with all good policy developments, it is to be recommended that students are invited to offer up their views in relation to the rules that they feel would benefit the class most in terms of achieving effective teaching and learning. A question such as, 'What rules would make it easier for you to learn?' would undoubtedly give rise to a lively student discussion or debate. Equally, inviting them to come up with a menu of rewards and sanctions will reinforce the sense of ownership that is so important to policy development, because the students are more likely to see the plan as theirs and, as a result, they will be more motivated to support it.

It is not uncommon for students to hold rules that are considerably stricter than that of their teachers. For this reason Canter and Canter would advise teachers to have a clear view of the rules that they wish to introduce before opening the discussion. Teachers can then guide their students more easily to the most appropriate and realistic rules.

Sample discipline plans for primary and post-primary students can be found in Canter and Canter's book. However, for convenience and as quick illustration I have made up a discipline plan, which can be seen in the Information Box below.

Information Box: Classroom Discipline Plan

To enable the teacher to teach and students to learn, a Classroom Discipline Plan has been formed for this class as follows:

Rules
- Students will arrive on time for lessons.
- Students will come to class properly equipped with the necessary material.
- Students will remain in their seats unless asked to move.
- Students will listen in silence when a teacher or student is speaking.
- Students will raise their hand and wait to be asked before speaking.
- Students will treat others, their work and their equipment with respect.

Rewards
- Praise/positive message.
- Positive message to share with parents.
- Special privilege.
- Special awards.

Consequences (Discipline Hierarchy)
- First offence: a warning.
- Second offence: a warning recorded by class teacher.
- Third offence: given a yellow card (may mean working away from the group for five to ten minutes or a detention, in keeping with the school's discipline code).
- Fourth offence: given a red card (may mean contacting parents or giving two detentions).
- Fifth offence: referral to the principal who can recommend, if deemed appropriate, suspension or expulsion.

The second step is to finalise the list of rules, rewards and corrective feedback and pass them by the principal to make sure there is nothing that conflicts with the school's code of behaviour. Ideally, the principal should encourage all staff to adopt assertive discipline. In this way it would help to establish a whole school approach to behaviour management that is positive and restorative.

The third step is to communicate the final discipline plan to the students and, preferably, to the parents. This will involve explaining to the students exactly how the plan will be implemented. They will learn, for example, that the discipline policy will give them the opportunity to exercise control and to take responsibility for their behaviour. In other words, it will be their choice that will determine the outcome. The discipline hierarchy clearly spells out what will happen from the first time a student breaks a rule to the fifth time the same student breaks a rule the same day. Students start with a clear slate each day, but there is scope to adjust this, provided all students are clear about the rules. Thus, any corrective action that has to be taken will be of their making, as they know only too well the consequences to that wrongdoing. It is this process that will lead to self-discipline, which is so much the key to success.

It is a good idea to display the discipline plan in the classroom. This will act as a constant reminder of the rules and what follows if they are broken. It may also act as an inspiration to colleagues to adopt a similar approach to classroom management.

The final step is to evoke the discipline plan. If we take the plan as shown in the Information Box above, it is to be expected that a lesson would run as follows:

1. Cormac, remember our rule, which is to remain in your seat unless you are asked to move. So you have now received a warning.
2. Cormac, this is the second time that I have had to correct you for not staying in your seat. This is a reminder, so you have chosen to have your name written into my incident book.
3. Cormac, this is the third time that you have broken our class rules, this time for speaking out of turn when you should be reading. You have chosen to receive a yellow card.

It should be noted that there will probably always be some students who will resist until they learn that you mean what you say. The important principle is to remain calm, as being angry, sarcastic or demeaning is counterproductive. Corrective actions are not meant to punish students; rather, they are, as Canter and Canter stress, 'intended to stop the disruptive behaviour and to remind the students that it is in their own interest to choose more appropriate behaviour'. Therefore, all that teachers need to do is calmly but firmly and consistently tell disruptive students what they are supposed to do and to follow this by mentioning the corrective action they will receive.

Exceptions to the Rule

While consistency is a key to the success of the discipline plan, with students knowing that misbehaviour carries with it a corrective action every single time, it is recognised that occasions will arise when teachers will need to exercise their own professional judgement rather than blindly follow the discipline hierarchy. As the goal is to establish a positive and caring relationship with all students, it may not always be in the student's best interest to receive corrective action. This may, for example, be the case when a student is extremely upset or angry, or the behaviour is totally out of character. In such circumstances, Canter and Canter recommend that if teachers are unsure how to respond, a good rule of thumb would be to ask themselves, 'How would I want my own child to be treated in this situation?'

Recognising Positive Behaviour

Once a student's behaviour has been corrected, it is important to grasp the first opportunity there is to recognise the student's positive behaviour. 'Catching them when they're good' should be the motto. Remarking, for example, 'Cormac, you handled that really well', will not only reinforce the positive behaviour, but will do wonders for building a positive pupil-teacher relationship and promote self-esteem. As one student remarked in an article on assertive discipline: 'Teachers only used to be interested if you were naughty, now they notice us all the time.' The article also reported how a school secretary said: 'Three years ago local people complained about pupil behaviour. Now they tell us how good they are. I live around here and I feel proud.'[7]

Assertive discipline, in addition to rewarding individual students, also encourages classwide supportive feedback. So when the class as a whole has been behaving and working to an optimal standard, a class reward can be given, for example, a special treat, time given over to an activity of the students' choice or a choice of homework. A recognition system for the whole class is extremely effective because it makes use of peer pressure. Students will remind each other to follow instructions and behave so they do not miss out on a class reward. The technique shows students how important it is to work together in a co-operative manner in order to achieve a common goal. According to Canter and Canter, the class reward system is best used during the first month of school to establish 'following directions' in a co-operative way. It should be discontinued and brought back only to work on a specific problem or during, for example, the last month of each term.

Generally, the students would be clear on what is expected of them (for example, carrying out an assignment) and how many points are needed to get a class reward. Incidentally, younger children enjoy having marbles dropped into a jar instead of working with points. The length of time that it takes to earn the total points/marbles that are needed to qualify for a reward can vary from one day to two weeks, depending on the age of the students.

The way it works is that whenever the teacher sees the students, or at least a significant number of them, following the directions given (for example, I want you all to take out your maths books now and try questions five to ten), a point will be awarded, which can be logged on the board or on a chart, or if marbles are used, one can be dropped into a jar. When the class has earned the right amount the reward is given.

A Team Approach

There is no reason why assertive discipline cannot be used in a similar manner to that of the 'Good Behaviour' game. Some readers may be familiar with this approach, which has been used to good effect since it was introduced in the late 1960s to help reduce disruptive behaviour. The procedure divides the class into teams, normally two. The teacher specifies the misbehaviours (leaving one's seat, talking out of turn, engaging in disruptive behaviour) and when anyone violates the rule, the team receives a penalty point. The team with the fewest penalty points or any team with fewer than the specified number of marks receive a number of privileges (line up first for lunch, choose an activity for the class). If adapted to fit the assertive discipline model, the team with the most positive points for good behaviour wins.

Misbehaviour that Occurs Outside of the Classroom

It is to be expected that misbehaviour that occurs outside of the classroom will be dealt with according to the schoolwide discipline plan and, therefore, it should not conflict with a teacher's individual discipline plan. However, it is to be hoped that the schoolwide discipline plan would incorporate the same principles as that of assertive discipline, thus promoting clarity and consistency around the rules and the consequences if any of them are broken.

For further information on delivering assertive discipline and integrating this form of behaviour management and teaching to great effect, I highly recommend the third edition of *Lee Canter's Assertive Discipline* by Lee Canter and Marlene Canter. Another great source is Bill Roger's book, *Behaviour Management: A Whole-School Approach.*[8] It complements assertive discipline, putting forward the same principles, and offers good practical suggestions to help with developing whole school strategies for dealing with student behaviour.

Key Messages

- Effective classroom discipline is an essential component to a whole school approach to bullying prevention.
- Lee Canter's assertive discipline provides an ideal tool for managing student behaviour, while at the same time promoting responsible behaviour and fostering positive student-teacher relationships.
- Assertive discipline takes the stress and strain out of teaching and learning. It allows teachers to establish a discipline plan made up of (1) rules for the class to follow, (2) supportive feedback for following the rules and (3) corrective actions when students choose not to follow the rules.
- Assertive discipline allows teachers to model fair, consistent and respectful behaviour. The emphasis on rules lets students know what behaviours are expected of them. The emphasis on supportive feedback encourages positive behaviours, increases student's self-esteem and promotes a positive classroom environment in which to learn. Corrective actions are dealt with calmly, quickly and consistently, and are balanced with positive support.
- Assertive discipline can be adapted to suit a teacher's individual style and philosophy of teaching, giving expression to their creativity and resourcefulness.

Notes

1. See, for example, 'When the Bully Starts Abusing the Teacher', *Irish Times*, 18 October 1994, and 'Half of all Primary Teachers "bullied"', *Irish Times*, 12 March 2007.

2. Department of Education and Science, *School Matters: The Report of the Task Force on Student Behaviour in Second Level Schools*, 2006.

3. *Irish Times*, 2 April 2010.

4. Munn, P. (ed.), *Promoting Positive Discipline: Whole School Approaches to Tackling Low Level Disruption*, Edinburgh: Scottish Office, 1999.

5. www.vista-europe.org.

6. Canter, L. and Canter, M., *Lee Canter's Assertive Discipline: Positive Behaviour Management For Today's Classroom*, Los Angeles: Canter and Associates, Inc., 2001.

7. *Observer*, 8 March 1993.

8. Rogers, B., *Behaviour Management: A Whole-School Approach,* London: Paul Chapman, 2004.

10 DEALING WITH BULLYING BEHAVIOUR (TRADITIONAL AND CYBER)

Sooner or later every teacher has to deal with incidents of bullying, whether of a traditional or cyber nature. They may be a witness to bullying behaviour or they may receive reports of bullying from victims, bystanders, parents or others in the school community. How incidents of bullying are dealt with will send out strong messages not only to the students involved, but also to the whole school community. It is, therefore, vital that teachers take each incident seriously and deal with it appropriately. Teachers need to be seen to take action, otherwise students are under the impression that teachers do not care or do not consider bullying sufficiently important to justify corrective feedback.

In Part One, I reported that whereas the majority of teachers felt that they tried to stop bullying that came to their attention, almost half of the pupils felt this was not the case. Whatever the reason for this discrepancy in viewpoints, or whether each party defines bullying differently, the important fact is that any lack of action on the part of teachers leaves students with the impression that their teachers do not take bullying seriously. This is most unfortunate, as it serves to discourage students, bystanders and even parents from bringing complaints of bullying to the attention of school staff. Quite apart from denying a victim support, it mitigates against the very climate of 'telling', which is such a key component in promoting a whole school approach to bullying. It also lets the aggressors off the hook with lost opportunity to correct their behaviour.

Responding to Reports of Bullying

The Cool School Programme (*Responding to Bullying: First Steps for Teachers*)[1] advises the following steps when a student tells a teacher that he/she is being bullied.

1. Listen

Attend to what is being said without displaying shock or disbelief. For a victim to come forward can take a lot of courage and insofar as it is often a cry for help, it deserves a supportive response. Allow the victim time to tell their story. Be patient and wait during silences, prompting gently if necessary. To allow the victim as much privacy as possible it is to be recommended that some quiet place be found, be it an office or empty classroom.

2. Take Notes

Jot down notes as these can form the basis of a report for dealing with the incident. In keeping with best practice, the notes and any cyber evidence (e-mails, voice mails, text messages, 'happy slapping' film clips) should also be kept on file as part of the school's bullying records. They will serve the school well should a legal case ever arise.

When taking notes it is advisable to use the student's own words as much as possible. This avoids the temptation to interpret events. Notes should also be taken of the non-verbal behaviour, for example, did he/she present as upset, angry or depressed? In addition, efforts should be made to include details of:

- the nature of the incident;
- the names of those involved;
- the names of witnesses;
- the date, time, place.

Leading questions should be avoided, for example, 'What did he/she do then?' Instead, use open questions such as, 'Do you have anything else on your mind that you wish to tell me?'

3. Allay Fears and Provide Reassurance

In view of the fears that surround telling, such as fear of reprisals or not being believed (see p. 48), it is critical that students who tell, whether victim or bystander, are reassured that he/she was right to tell. Telling is behaving in a praiseworthy, responsible and honourable manner. In addition, a victim who tells should be told that:

- action will be taken to stop the bullying;
- bullying can happen to anyone, and nobody should have to put up with it;
- bullying is unacceptable and the problem lies with the aggressor.

4. Ensure the Student's Safety

Steps need to be taken to ensure the immediate safety of the student to limit and prevent further harm. This is especially the case if there are threats of physical or sexual assaults. If the student is at risk of assault on the way home from school ('You'll pay for this you rat, I'll get you after school'), parents should be called or some other arrangements made to safeguard the student. Long-term support may also need to be considered. This can include the school counsellors or pastoral staff and external specialist agencies where appropriate. However, it is paramount that no time is lost in apprehending the aggressors. The sooner they know that a teacher is on to them and that action will be taken the better for everyone concerned. If the bullying behaviour is of a very disturbing nature (for example, sexual or physical), care needs to be taken that the behaviour is not underpinned by abuse taking place at the home of the perpetrator or in some other setting. If this were to be the case, the perpetrator will also need safeguarding, to the extent that civil authorities should be informed, in accordance with the national guidelines.[2]

5. Negotiate Confidentiality

Fearful of being labelled a snitch or a rat, victims and, indeed, bystanders need to be reassured that matters will be dealt with in as sensitive and confidential a manner as possible in order to achieve a positive outcome. Restorative approaches are especially good at diminishing the fear and guilt that is associated with blowing the whistle on bullying (see Chapter 11). It is important to note, however, that where one is responding to a report of sexist, sexual or transphobic bullying, issues of confidentiality and disclosing sensitive information can become a very pertinent issue.[3] The most recent 'Quick Guide' issued by the UK Department for Children, Schools and Families on *Guidance for Schools on Preventing and Responding to Sexist, Sexual and Transphobic Bullying* recommend that, 'The school's confidentiality policy should provide a framework for staff when deciding whether or not they can offer confidentiality to a pupil who discloses information about themselves or their situation.'

6. Tell the Student you will Keep in Contact

Victims and all who may bring bullying to the attention of staff should be given some idea as to how the complaint will be dealt with. Follow-up feedback is also of paramount importance as it reassures the parties concerned that bullying is treated seriously. No parent, for example, should be left in the dark after having reported an incident of bullying, as it causes unnecessary agitation and worry for them and their child. It is better to keep victimised students and parents informed of developments, even if they are slow, and give them an 'open door' if they need to talk.

7. Make the Intervention

The school's anti-bullying policy should dictate how to proceed with a report of bullying, whether it is of a traditional or cyber nature. It is common practice that if it is of a serious nature it is referred to the principal straight away. Some schools may choose to have dedicated staff (the anti-bullying committee) take charge of resolving allegations of bullying.

In any event, in responding to a report of bullying, be it from a victim, parent or bystander, I recommend that action is taken as quickly as possible. However, decisions will need to be made as to whom to consult in order to gain as much information as possible about the incident. It is extremely helpful to talk to witnesses of the event. When the moment comes to apprehend the alleged perpetrator(s), it is advisable to proceed as follows:

- Decide whether to interview alleged aggressors separately or together and whether one wishes to be guided in doing so by the 'No Blame Approach' and the 'Common Concern Method' (see information relating to both methods in Chapter 11).
- Remain calm. Avoid an accusatory tone. Reacting emotionally may add to the aggressor's fun and strengthen his/her ability to manipulate and control a situation. Reacting aggressively or punitively gives a message that it is alright to be aggressive if you have the power.

- Do not criticise the aggressor in personal terms, only their behaviour.
- It is not necessary to tell the aggressor who has reported the incident, only that the incident has come to the attention of the school authorities.
- Assure the aggressor that his or her side of the story will be heard before a decision is made.
- Take notes using a reporting form, as with the victim (see Information Box on p. 147).
- Consider using a restorative approach such as mediation, the 'No Blame Approach' or the 'Common Concern Method' (see Chapter 11).
- If bullying is upheld, the perpetrator(s) should be informed:
  o that his or her behaviour constituted an unambiguous incident of bullying behaviour, and that this is in breach of school policy;
  o that he or she must refrain from all forms of bullying in future;
  o that he or she apologise either in person or in writing to the victim;
  o that an agreement is reached as to how he or she intends to behave towards the victim;
  o that, in future, specified sanctions, in line with the anti-bullying policy, will be implemented should there be further instances;
  o that acts of retribution against the victim will be dealt with by one of the severest possible sanctions. In accordance with best practice, the sanctions should already be clear to the students. If it is a first offence, a reminder of the sanctions should be given, in other words, a warning like the yellow and red cards used in the assertive discipline philosophy.

It should be noted that there will be many occasions when teachers will see students in the act of bullying with their own eyes. This requires immediate action so that no one is under any illusion that the behaviour is in any way condoned. In dealing with students caught bullying, the aim is to:

- stop the bullying behaviour immediately;
- change the student's attitude and shape his/her behaviour for the future;

- reconcile the pupils involved, if possible;
- restore harmony.

My recommendations for how teachers might react on the spot when witnessing an act of bullying can be seen in the Information Box below.

Information Box: Teachers' Immediate Response to Bullying

- Remain calm. Reacting emotionally may add to the bully's fun and strengthen his ability to control a situation. Also, reacting aggressively or punitively gives the message that it is alright to bully if you have the power.
- Take the incident seriously. Ask: who, what, why, where, when?
- Take action as quickly as possible.
- Decide whether your action needs to be private or public; who are the pupils involved?
- Reassure the victim(s), don't make them feel inadequate or foolish.
- Offer concrete help, advice and support to the victim.
- Make it plain to the bully that you disapprove.
- Encourage the bully to see the victim's point of view.
- Set realistic, firm and consistent guidelines to help the child control his/her behaviour.
- Ensure that the child apologises, either in person or in writing, to the child he/she bullied.
- Consider using either the 'No Blame Approach' or the 'Common Concern Method'.
- Punish the bully if you have to, but be very careful HOW you do this.

(Anti-Bullying Centre, Trinity College Dublin)

---

8. Support Strategies for those Involved in Bullying Behaviour

As I have stated, a whole school approach to bullying prevention should include the development of support strategies (mentorship schemes, counselling, social skills training, assertiveness training, anger management and anger replacement training), which may help those involved in bullying, as victims, as bullies or both. For example, where counselling may be the preferred option for a 'pure victim', social skills work may be the answer for students who are persistent anti-social perpetrators or, indeed, a 'provocative victim'. In each case, as was pointed out by the authors of *Dealing With Bullying in Schools*:[4] 'The student concerned may have (and perhaps is unaware of) a personal interactive style that increases his or her propensity to be involved in situations of bullying behaviour. Such a person's awareness of how he or she relates to and interacts with others can be gently pointed out, and new social strategies can be suggested and taught by a classroom staff member with an appropriate pastoral role.'

In addition, account needs to be taken of the fact that not everyone who has been found to bully is aware of the negative impact of their behaviour, i.e. the level of hurt caused. Also, there will be those who may feel unable to control their emotions when aroused. For those lacking in empathy, for example, empathy training should be an option, as should anger management training for those lacking in impulse control. Again, additional behaviour management strategies may be necessary for children who have been diagnosed with ADD or ADHD to deal with their impulsivity, which may result in them hitting out or being offensive without any apparent or intended provocation. For more detail on children with ADHD, see Elizabeth Nixon.[5]

Depending on size and budget, there is only so much expertise any one school can have. However, if schools have teachers who have professional qualifications to deal with social and emotional problems, this can make a real difference to helping victims and bullies overcome their social or emotional difficulties. If schools do not have such expertise, they would do well to consider seeking volunteers who might sign up to gaining professional expertise in some of the more commonly sought after support strategies. This would most certainly prevent the need to refer students to services outside of school where the chances of being seen in a speedy fashion are slim.

9. Referring Students who are in Need of Specialised Support
In dealing with students involved in bullying, it will become clear to teachers and principals that there are 'bullies', 'victims' and 'bully-victims' who are in need of tertiary prevention, that is, support that goes beyond what the school itself can provide to deal with persistent bullying. Referral, for example, may need to be made to the Educational Psychology Services, Child/Family Guidance Services or Professional Counselling Services. Equally, if there is a case of possible suspension or expulsion, I would prefer to see that the student and parents are given the choice by the principal (and the Board of

Management, if involved) as to whether they wish to have the sanction imposed or to seek help instead, such as counselling, social skills training, anger management or assertiveness training, from a professional external body. Naturally, if parents choose the latter course, it would be on condition that they furnish the school with evidence that their child/teenager is attending and receiving the necessary therapy. If the help given can turn the child/teenager around to behaving positively, there is much the school can be proud of in terms of helping that individual student to achieve his/her potential in school and society.

10. Make a Record

For future reference and if there should ever be a legal case over a bullying incident, teachers who investigate cases of bullying are well advised to keep a written record of their discussions with those involved. It may also be appropriate to ask those involved to write down their account of the situation. The development of a reporting form, such as the one illustrated below, is also useful. It allows for the easy recording of:

- details from interviews with victims and perpetrators;
- details from witness statements;
- the nature of agreements that are made with those involved in an incident, including parents;
- any action taken by the school, for example, the 'No Blame Approach', mediation, sanctions, referral to counselling or psychological help.

The students involved should be asked to sign the form. If parents are involved, they should also be asked to sign it so all are clear on the nature of the agreement. For other practical tools that teachers may wish to use to prevent and counter bullying, consult www.antibullyingcampaign.ie. The tools are downloadable free of charge.

Sample Reporting Form

Pupil's name: ....

Class:................................Teacher: ....

Who reported the incident?...

....

Where did this happen?..

....

Behaviour displayed: bullying................. Being bullied: ....

Physical bullying: yes/no

If yes, please give details:...

....

Verbal bullying: yes/no

If yes, please give details:...

....

Comments: ....

....

Actions taken: Date: / /

....

Follow-up: Date: / /

....

Parent's signature   ....

Teacher's signature   ....

(Anti-Bullying Centre, Trinity College Dublin)

Guidelines for Talking to Parents

With the increased concern about bullying and the heightened awareness of the association of suicide and bullying, the most recent account being that of fifteen-year-old Phoebe Prince,[6] it is to be expected that parents may more readily than before contact teachers with their concerns about bullying. It is not uncommon for parents to become very emotional, especially if they sense the response to be defensive.[7] A sensitive approach is therefore needed, as will be the case when there is a need to contact the parents of the alleged perpetrator(s).

Talking to Parents of a Child/Teenager Who is Being Bullied

- Allow the parent(s) to express their feelings freely without interrupting.
- Accept their feelings. They are real for the parent, even though they might seem excessive.
- Assure the parent(s) that you are pleased that they have taken the time to see you.

147

- Stress that bullying is unacceptable (hopefully there is a strong school policy statement to back this up) and that you intend to take action.
- Assure them that you will keep in touch with them. There is nothing that will anger parents more than to hear nothing back after a complaint has been made.

Parents of a Child/Teenager Who has Bullied

- Avoid labelling the student as a bully. Begin by offering some positive view/aspect of the student.
- Show genuine concern for the student's problem (anti-social bullying behaviour) and a concern to help that student fulfil his/her potential. Useful phrases include, 'I'm sure we both share concern for X's future' and, 'We need to help him/her to show his/her best side/develop his/her potential and talents'.
- Inquire if there is anything that could be upsetting the student or triggering the bullying behaviour.
- Persuade the parent(s) to agree, if possible, that being aggressive towards a child who bullies is counterproductive. What is needed is a positive and constructive approach with firm and consistent limits (suggestions to assist parents in helping their child/teenager refrain from bullying can be found in Chapter 15).
- Explain what you intend to do next and get their agreement, if possible.
- Promise (and do) keep in touch to update the parent(s) on the situation.

Key Messages

- Prevent bullying by addressing all acts of inappropriate aggression.
- Take a non-judgemental and calm approach as you inform yourself of a case of bullying, setting an example of how to deal with conflict.
- Talk to all involved in the bullying: the aggressors, victims, bystanders and, if necessary, the parents.
- Make a record of what was said by those interviewed and the actions which were decided upon. Have the record signed by all involved as an accurate record of events.
- If allegations of bullying are upheld, apply the sanctions that are laid down in the school's anti-bullying policy.

- Consider using a restorative approach to deal with the bullying, for example, the 'No Blame Approach' or mediation (see Chapter 6).
- Ensure that the causative factors for both victim and bully (social skills deficiencies, low self-esteem, poor tolerance for frustration) are dealt with.
- Do not hesitate to work with parents or guardians and professional agencies to correct behaviours causative of victimisation and bullying.

Notes

1. Cool School Programme, *Responding To Bullying: First Steps for Teachers*, North Eastern Health Board, Ireland, 2001.
2. Children First National Guidelines for the Protection and Welfare of Children, Office of the Minister for Children and Youth Affairs, 1999.
3. Guidance for schools on preventing and responding to sexist, sexual and transphobic bullying: *Safe to Learn: Embedding Anti-Bullying Work in Schools. Quick Guide*, Department for Children, Schools and Families, 2009 (http://publications.education.gov.uk).
4. 'The Big Story: Bullied to Death', *Sunday Independent*, 14 March 2010.
5. Gleeson, C., 'School Left My Son to Suffer in Silence', *Irish Independent*, 17 May 2010.
6. O'Moore, M. and Minton, S.J., *Dealing With Bullying in Schools: A Training Manual for Teachers, Parents and Other Professionals*, London: Paul Chapman, 2004.
7. Nixon, E., 'The Social Competence of Children with Attention Hyperactivity Disorder: A Review of the Literature' in *Child Psychology & Psychiatry Review*, 6 (2001), pp. 172–180.

RESTORATIVE APPROACHES TO BULLYING (TRADITIONAL AND CYBER)

In Chapter 3, I put forward the rationale for promoting restorative rather than punitive approaches. For the same reason that physical punishment was withdrawn from schools because of its ineffectiveness, a case can also be made not to subject those who bully to punitive measures. In *Psychology Applied to Teaching*,[1] we learn that 'the weight of laboratory evidence suggests that punishment is ineffective in modifying behaviour' because:

- mild punishment is ineffective;
- punished behaviour recurs when the punisher is not present;
- what seems to be punishment may actually be reinforcing attention;
- punishment produces side effects that interfere with learning (fear, anxiety, lowered self-esteem);
- punishers model the behaviours they sometimes wish to suppress (aggression);
- to be effective punishment needs to be immediate and relatively severe, which may conflict with legal and ethical standards.

Instead of punishment, ways must to be found in which corrective action is constructive and rehabilitative. This implies that the wrongs committed must be acknowledged and their impact understood. Ways to put things right must also be explored and decided upon. Closure is found when all those involved in the wrongdoing feel it has been dealt with fairly and satisfactorily.

Two relatively straightforward methods that teachers can easily adopt, which have all the characteristics of a restorative approach, are the 'No Blame Approach'[2] and the 'Common Concern Method'.[3] The No Blame Approach is increasingly being named the 'Support Group

Approach'.[4] This is because its original name became a source of conflict with those who did not appreciate that 'no blame' does not mean 'no responsibility'. In fact, the exact opposite is true. Some schools, therefore, refer to the No Blame Approach very appropriately as 'Taking Responsibility Approach'.

In effect, the 'no blame' philosophy offers an escape from the 'violence begets violence' cycle. Rather than trying to justify one's wrongdoing and feeling vengeful for being caught out, the No Blame Approach affords the offender the opportunity to learn new behaviours that will not only prevent further hurt to his/her victim, but also to him/herself should the 'tit for tat' campaign continue.

The No Blame Approach
When bullying has been observed or reported, a teacher wishing to adopt the No Blame Approach should carry out the following steps.

1. Interview the Victim
When the teacher finds out that bullying has happened they start by talking to the victim to learn how he/she feels. It does not need to be a fact-finding mission, but it is important for the victim to say who was involved. The victim should be told that the intervention will be a non-punitive one, as that will help to ease any fear of further victimisation that the victim may have.

2. Convene a Meeting with the People Involved
The teacher arranges to meet with the group of pupils who have been involved. This will include some bystanders or colluders who joined in but did not initiate the bullying. A group of six to eight works well.

3. Explain the Position
The teacher tells the group about the way the victim is feeling and a poem or piece of writing or drawing of theirs may be used to emphasise the distress. At no time does the teacher discuss the details of the incidents or allocate blame to the group.

4. Share Responsibility

The teacher does not attribute blame but states that he/she knows that the group are responsible and can do something about it.

5. Ask the Group for Their Ideas

Each student of the group is encouraged to suggest a way in which the victim could be helped to feel happier. The teacher gives some positive response, but he/she does not go on to extract a promise of improved behaviour.

6. Leave it Up to Them

The teacher ends the meeting by passing over the responsibility to the group to solve the problem. A further meeting with the group is arranged in order to monitor the student's progress.

7. Meet Them Again

About a week later, the teacher meets with each student individually, including the victim, to review their progress giving them the opportunity to report back on their contribution to resolving the problem. This enables the teacher to monitor the bullying and to keep the students involved in the process. The authors note that it is not critical if everyone has not kept to his/her intention, as long as the bullying has stopped.

A Special Note

The UK anti-bullying pack for schools, *Bullying: Don't Suffer in Silence*, reports that over a two-year period, 80 per cent of cases in primary schools were dealt with successfully without a delay by applying a (very slight) adaptation of the No Blame Approach. The victim, they state, continued to experience bullying in only 6 per cent of cases. Results in secondary schools were similar. The steps of the Support Group Approach, as adapted from the No Blame Approach, can be seen in the Information Box below.

Information Box: The Support Group Approach (Recommended from age nine)

- The teacher talks with the victim and a support group made up of six to eight students. As well as the students involved in the bullying, friends of the victim can also take part.

- With the agreement of the victim, the victim's feelings are shared with the group. The teacher stresses that the purpose of the meeting is to take responsibility and find a solution. Suggestions on how to help are sought, but the key aim is a joint commitment to take action.
- A week later each student in the group is interviewed individually to see how things are going. The bullied pupil is also seen. While some students might not have fully kept to their good intentions, the main criterion for success is that the bullying has stopped.

The Common Concern Method (Anatol Pikas of Sweden, 1989)

I first learnt about the Common Concern Method when it was in its infancy at the first European Seminar on School Bullying.[5] The method is very similar to the No Blame Approach and the Support Group Approach; indeed, both are adaptations of Pikas' Common Concern Method. It differs in only small ways. Essentially, those involved in bullying are spoken to individually, starting with the ring leader. The victim is interviewed after all the perpetrators have been seen and offered a solution as to how they intend to start behaving towards the victim.

The therapeutic dialogue would proceed as follows:

No-blame start: 'I understand that you have been bullying Mary.'
Request information: 'Tell me what has been going on?'
Seek solutions: 'What can you do to improve the situation? What do you suggest?' The aim is to achieve at least a respectful relationship, if becoming friends is unrealistic.
Agree and arrange a follow-up meeting: agree some constructive approach or action (for example, apologise, be friendly and influence friends to be so also). Arrange a time for the next meeting.
Review meeting: 'Can you tell me how you have been getting on since we last met?'

Pikas believes that interviewing the perpetrators first helps to protect the victim from the risk of retaliation. Incidentally, he states that he and his collaborators have hardly ever met a victim who is reluctant to talk. If anything, the victims talk with relief and even pleasure.

As with the other no blame/support group approaches, each of the perpetrators are met individually at regular intervals to review their progress. When the staff member or counsellor in charge of the process is happy that their behaviour has changed to reflect positive behaviour towards the victim, they are all brought together as a group. At the group meeting, preferably seated in a circle, they discuss the bullied person and comment positively about him/her. When the facilitator of the group judges the moment is right, he/she invites the victim to join the group (the victim is best seated beside the facilitator). The group is then invited to express the positive feelings that they may now have for the victim. The group is praised for turning their behaviour around and stopping the bullying. However, they are reminded that they will be checked up on again, in a week or one month's time, for reassurance of their continuing positive behaviour.

If the victim is a provocative one, with the perpetrators feeling somewhat justified that the victim is his/her worst enemy and therefore to blame, the process will naturally take longer. It is anticipated that there will be a few group meetings before the group is ready to meet with the provocative victim. By the time they meet with the victim, it is anticipated that the victim, with the help of the facilitator/counsellor, will have gained some insight into his/her provocative behaviour. At the final meeting, each former perpetrator is invited to express in positive and sincere terms their opinion about the victim, who simply listens. The facilitator, acting in this case as a mediator, then asks the victim what he/she has to say about what he/she has just heard. Any further unresolved problems will be mediated in such a way that allows both victim and former perpetrators to find ways of living together.

A Special Note

According to Pikas, from his experience, teachers who adopt his Common Concern Approach in dealing with bullying develop, with few exceptions, the ability and willingness to deal constructively not only with their teaching, but with people in general.

Mediation

Mediation is highly regarded as a restorative approach in that it is not about deciding who is right, apportioning blame or even focusing on the past any more than is necessary. This technique helps the disputants to work out a way forward that is mutually acceptable to both parties. It is about finding a win-win solution. It can be used very effectively by both students and teachers, although not all incidents of school bullying will be amenable to mediation. This is particularly true when there is a great power differential between the victim and bully. In some cases, mediation may also need to be backed up by other intervention strategies, including sanctions.

I will be introducing peer mediation later on in the book when I focus on peer support strategies, but for now I will outline how teachers can best put mediation into practice. The steps to be taken by an adult, which are outlined in *Bullying: Don't Suffer in Silence* (referred to earlier), are as follows:

- Hold brief, non-confrontational, individual 'chats' with each student in a quiet room without interruptions, starting with the bullying students.
- Get agreement with each that the bullied student is unhappy and that they will help improve the situation. If they cannot do this, be prescriptive.
- Chat supportively with the bullied student, helping them to understand how to change if they are thought to have provoked the bullying.
- Check progress a week later, then meet all involved to reach agreement on reasonable long-term behaviour. At this stage participants usually cease bullying.
- Check whether the bullying starts again or targets another pupil.
- If bullying persists, combine the method with some other action targeted specifically at that student, such as parental involvement or a change of class.

For schools to use mediation to good effect, staff training is vital. It is also beneficial if more than one member of staff, including non-teaching staff, is trained because this avoids one person from being 'typecast'. It would also be valuable to invite parents to training sessions. Indeed, it would be great if schools could arrange classes for parents to learn conflict resolution skills and mediation. If children can, as I have shown, transfer skills learned in school to their homes and neighbourhood to prevent and counter conflict, there is no reason why the same cannot be true of parents.

Restorative Conferencing

Restorative conferencing in schools seeks to repair more serious harm that has been caused between members of the school community.[6] It has the ability to settle disputes not only between students, but also between student and teacher or between parent and teacher. This process usually involves both victim and perpetrator and their parents/supporters, as well as key members of staff. They are invited to attend the conference by the facilitator and the procedure is very similar to mediation.

A study carried out by the UK Youth Justice Board (2004) found most encouraging results among primary and post-primary schools when conferencing is systematically implemented and becomes embedded in the whole school approach to bullying prevention. Conferencing was used to deal with anti-social behaviour, bullying, violence and, indeed, truancy and exclusion. There was high satisfaction among both students and staff with 92 per cent of conferences resulting in lasting agreements between the parties involved. Marked changes in attitudes and behaviour of students were also found.[7] The steps are as follows:

- The facilitator talks to all involved before the conference to prepare them for the process and to answer any concerns that they may have. The conference can only go ahead if all involved agree to take part.
- Everyone taking part is invited to sit in a circle in a quiet room, free of interruptions.
- The ground rules are explained, for example, to establish the harm caused; to determine the emotional context and impact; to discover why the harm was done; to clarify what needs to be done to put things right; to make clear that there will be no repetition of the offending behaviour; to expect all at the conference to contribute to finding a way forward.
- Once the guidelines are established, the harm caused is presented for discussion. Each person is asked to set out exactly what happened,

how they felt then and how they feel now, starting with the victim(s) and followed by the perpetrator(s). It is important that the facilitator, in asking questions to gain as much information as possible, takes on a neutral, non-judgemental tone.

- When the victim(s) and the perpetrator(s) have given their accounts, the facilitator invites the others present to speak (the parents and school representatives).
- The facilitator gives autonomy to the group but is watchful that no one is ignored or showing signs of distress or anger, in which case some intervention may be necessary.
- Acknowledge what took place at the meeting and the steps which were agreed upon. If appropriate, a follow-up meeting can be arranged. Reparation can also mean, if appropriate, involvement in some rehabilitative programme, like counselling or aggression replacement training (ART).

The most useful resources of restorative conferencing include case study material. Below is one such case study, presented by Dobrinka Chankova and Tanya Poshtovain in VISTA,[8] which illustrates the positive outcomes of conferencing, in this case family group conferencing.

Case Study

The Incident

Christian, a tenth-grade student, is always well dressed, has a state-of-the-art mobile phone and every morning goes to school in his father's car. He never misses a chance to point out his new gains and utterly despises, completely neglects, those who cannot afford his standard. An especially frequent object of his sneers is Ivan, who comes from a poor family and lives in a remote neighbourhood. While Ivan is an excellent student, Christian is one of the academically weakest in the class. One day, after Christian's serial insulting words, calling him an 'outsider', Ivan cannot stand it any longer and answers back to Christian that his father's millions will not help him in any way and that Christian is and will remain the most stupid student in the class. The fight that follows ends with minor injuries to Christian and a broken leg to Ivan.

The Process

The school psychologist decides a reaction is needed and summons a family group conference. The following people take part in the conference: Ivan and his mother, Christian and his father, their class teacher and a friend of each of the students in conflict.

Ivan and his family are very upset by the incident; their dignity is deeply hurt. To make matters worse it is winter and commuting to school is problematic. Christian and his father feel awkward about the situation.

The class teacher is worried that the atmosphere in the class is very tense, the class is polarised and the verbal attacks between the differentiated groups continue and run the risk of growing into new forms of aggression.

The friends of the two classmates admit these facts as each insists on his own interpretation. The school psychologist is of the opinion that measures have to be taken to ease the class tension.

The Outcome

After discussions between the parents and among all the people together, the following plan of action is achieved:

1. Both students express regret for what has happened, apologise for the insulting words they have exchanged and engage to restrain from similar behaviour in the future.
2. Christian's father undertakes to drive Ivan to and from school until his recovery.
3. In his free time, Ivan will help Christian with his studies.
4. The class teacher will organise a discussion of the incident in class, where Ivan and Christian will declare that they have settled their differences and agree that they will not let similar incidents occur in the future.

Circle Time

Circle Time is probably the best known and to date the most widely used of all restorative approaches in schools, both primary and post-primary. The strategy is particularly useful when there are issues of concern, such as bullying, which need attention, or an event that has caused distress to the whole group. For twenty to thirty minutes, the teacher facilitates a safe and positive environment in which students take turns (if they wish) to talk about the issue that is presented. As in all restorative approaches, the members of the circle are encouraged to listen to each other carefully and discuss issues in a constructive and problem-solving way.

I believe that Circle Time would work very well in conjunction with a sociometric assessment. Those familiar with the Cool School Programme will know that a sociometric assessment is a most useful tool for coming to grips with the relationships in a class or group, for example, who are the popular students and who are the socially rejected. Very simply, each class member is asked a few questions designed to uncover the social dynamic in the class. Typical questions might be, 'Who do you like to work with?' and, 'Who would you like to have sitting beside you in class?' Each member of the class can, for example, be asked to write down three names of those in their class or group whom they would most like to be with in the situations specified. Were it felt to be appropriate, students can also be asked to name those they would dislike to be with. Great care needs to be taken with the latter approach to avoid feelings of humiliation of students who may be rejected.

Both acceptance and rejection scores can be plotted in the form of a sociogram, which has each child's name entered on a gram, with an arrow pointing towards the chosen student and showing who the nomination came from. The sociogram will then enable teachers to identify the popular, the average, the controversial, the neglected and the rejected. It will also identify cliques and subgroups who interact with each other.[9]

The information gained from a sociogram can then be used to good effect in Circle Time to develop a more inclusive and supportive climate among the students, where there is greater tolerance and respect for diversity. In addition to resolving specific problems, Circle Time has shown itself to be valuable in helping to develop self-esteem, appreciation of others, conflict management and problem-solving skills. Above all it has the potential to develop valuable relational and restorative experience and skills among all the members of the school community.

Aggression Replacement Training (ART)

Aggression replacement training is a three-pronged approach to dealing with chronically aggressive youth. Because of the multiple causes of aggression, both individual and societal, the authors of *Aggression Replacement Training*[10] are of the opinion that quick-fix programmes are of limited value. For this reason they have developed a programme for schools and other agencies that they feel gets to the heart of the deficiencies that cause aggressive behaviour. Their claim is that, first of all, aggressive youth lack many of the personal, interpersonal and social-cognitive skills that collectively make up effective pro-social behaviour. Secondly, their frequent impulsiveness and overreliance on aggressive behaviour to meet their daily needs and longer term goals reflects a deficiency in anger control. Thirdly, their tendency towards egocentric or selfish ways of behaving, disregarding rules and regulations, reflects a poor level of moral reasoning. For these reasons, the ART curriculum teaches a) skill streaming, b) anger control and c) moral reasoning.

Skill streaming is broken down into:

- Beginning social skills (listening, starting a conversation, asking a question, saying thank you).
- Advanced social skills (asking for help, joining in, giving instructions, apologising).
- Skills for dealing with feelings (expressing your feelings, understanding the feelings of others, dealing with fear).
- Skill alternatives to aggression (asking permission, negotiating, using self-control, standing up for your rights, responding to teasing, keeping out of fights).
- Skills for dealing with stress (dealing with being left out, responding to failure, dealing with embarrassment, dealing with group pressure).
- Planning skills (deciding on something to do, deciding on what caused a problem, setting a goal, concentrating on a task).

Anger control training teaches the A-B-C of anger:

A = What triggered the problem? What led up to it?
B = What did you do (the actual response to it)?
C = What were the consequences (for the victim and the aggressor)?

Keeping a hassle log or diary can help students gain an understanding of what triggers their aggression and the physical signs or cues that come over them (muscle tension, clenched fists, grinding teeth or a pounding heart). Knowing the triggers and the cues, they can then learn how to manage their anger (anger reducers) by using:

- Deep breathing (take a few deep, focusing breaths)
- Backward counting (count backwards from twenty to one)
- Pleasant imagery (conjure up a peaceful and relaxing scene).

Moral reasoning training attempts to remediate the moral disengagement, techniques of neutralisation and cognitive distortions, which so often characterise aggressive youth. Aggressive youth, for example, will often display immature reasoning by holding on to the view that 'might makes right', so much so that they disregard rules and disrespect viewpoints unless they are held by those more powerful than themselves.

Their immature morality is also reflected in their poor ability to understand the ideal of mutuality in a relationship, i.e. 'treat others as they wish to be treated themselves'. While probably present in all psychological disturbances, cognitive distortions that most often characterise easy-to-anger or chronically aggressive youths are:

- Ego-centric or self-centred thinking (when I get angry I don't care who gets hurt)
- Attributing hostile intent to others when none is intended, therefore assuming the worst (I caught him staring at me so I hit him)
- Blaming others or external forces for harmful actions (I had to bully her to keep in with my friends)
- Making little of an anti-social act (everyone sends nasty messages, it's no big deal)
- Blaming the victim (it was her fault for going out with the guy she knew I fancied).

It is clear that ART has much to offer a school when more serious measures are needed to curb students whose aggression, bullying and violence is very persistent and resistant to the usual discipline hierarchy that a school is able to offer. In Norway, some schools specialise in ART for students who have been withdrawn for their aggressive behaviour from mainstream education. Once they have learned to curb their aggression, they are returned to mainstream education.

It should be noted that while ART is designed for students who are persistent aggressors, there are exercises in social skills and assertiveness that would also benefit any victim of bullying who may be deficient in these skills. There is potential for individual as well as group training. Furthermore, students diagnosed with ADD or ADHD, who are involved as bully-victims or provocative victims, would clearly also benefit from ART training, which deals with social skills, assertiveness and impulse control.

While to teach ART would require some training, it would be an added bonus for a school if one or more teachers were to volunteer for such training. Any member of staff who is conversant with assertiveness training or social skills training would be well on the way to being a competent ART trainer. If students were able to avail of the ART programme or, indeed, just components of it, depending on the areas of deficiency that may be most causative of persistent aggression and bullying, it would undoubtedly cut down the need for suspensions and expulsions or referrals to a special school for behavioural and emotional difficulties.

For more details on ART, refer to *Aggression Replacement Training: A Comprehensive Intervention for Aggressive Youth*. In the book you will also find a very useful checklist, which teachers and parents can use to great effect to identify the social skills that are in need of correction.

Key Messages
- Wherever possible, use a restorative rather than a punitive approach to bullying.
- The No Blame Approach/Support Group Approach teaches children who bully to take responsibility for their behaviour and to make amends.
- The Common Concern Method is most effective when a gang or mob is involved in bullying.

- Mediation strengthens skills of conflict resolution and helps to restore positive relationships among the disputants.
- Restorative conferencing is effective in repairing more serious anti-social behaviour, bullying and violence.
- Circle Time facilitates a whole school approach and promotes a positive environment in which all views are expressed and solutions are sought.
- Aggression replacement therapy (ART) seeks to remediate deficiencies in social skills, anger control and moral reasoning.

Notes

1. Snowman, J. and Biehler, R., *Psychology Applied to Teaching*, 10th Edition, New York: Houghton Mifflin Company, 2003.

2. Maines, B. and Robinson, G., *The No Blame Approach*, Bristol: Lucky Duck Publishing, 1992.

3. Pikas, A., 'The Common Concern Method for the Treatment of Mobbing' in Roland, E. and Munthe, E. (eds), *Bullying: An International Perspective*, London: David Fulton, 1989.

4. Young, S., 'The Support Group Approach to Bullying in Schools', *Educational Psychology in Practice*, 14 (1998), pp. 32–39.

5. Pikas, op. cit.

6. Hopkins, B., *Just Schools: A Whole School Approach to Restorative Justice*, London: Jessica Kingsley Publishers, 2004.

7. Youth Justice Board for England and Wales, *Restorative Justice in Schools (Full Report) (D61)*, 2004.

8. See Chapter 5 in *School Bullying and Violence: Taking Action*: www.vistop.org/ebook.

9. For more details on the use of sociometric techniques, consult Banks and Thompson (1995) and Fontana (1995) in the Recommended Reading section, or Trinity College's Anti-Bullying Centre.

10. Goldstein, A.P., Glick, B. and Gibbs, J.C., *Aggression Replacement Training: A Comprehensive Intervention for Aggressive Youth*, Illinois: Research Press, 1998.

12 | PEER SUPPORT STRATEGIES

In Part One, I stressed the importance of empowering students to intervene when they witness acts of bullying among their peers. The majority of students are aware of the bullying incidents that occur and there is little doubt that their intervention would do much to diffuse or even stop the bullying. We know from our research that there are many bystanders who would like to help when they see someone being bullied, but they feel unable to do so due to fear or lack of confidence. Quite apart from being upset by what they see, many also carry guilt because of their inaction – a guilt that can last a lifetime.

Accepting that schools have a responsibility to ensure the safety of all their students, the key to achieving this is to have staff enlist the students' full support in stopping any bullying that they witness. For this to happen students will need to be properly informed about bullying and given the skills to intervene. There are a variety of programmes that have been designed to provide peer support in schools. They can be categorised into two broad groups. The first are those that are educational and which deepen the students' understanding of bullying, developing in them a greater individual and collective sense of responsibility to prevent and counter bullying among their peers. Among these schemes are co-operative group work, circle time, peer education, peer tutoring and mentoring.

The other group of peer support schemes are those that involve students playing an active and distinctive part in providing emotional support to victims, as well as helping to put an end to the bullying without teacher intervention.

In view of the fact that students prefer on the whole to sit down with their peers rather than with their teachers to resolve emotional issues, it is this latter group of peer support approaches that I believe holds great promise for schools. For this reason and for the fact that they are not widely used in schools as yet, I will now dwell on them in some more detail. They are:

- Befriending (from age seven)
- Circle of Friends (from age seven)
- School Watch (from age nine)
- Peer mediation (from age nine)
- Peer counselling (from age eleven)
- Peer mentoring (from age eleven)
- Cyber-mentors.

Befriending/Buddying

To say that friendship is a protective factor against bullying is probably an understatement. Having a number of friends and, indeed, a best friend can act as a powerful buffer and provide great protection against being bullied. Naturally important is the quality of the friendships, as is the status of the friends among their peers. The more loyal and the higher the standing of their friends, the more protected a student will be from becoming a victim.

Befriending is an approach not dissimilar to the Meitheal programme promoted by Brendan Byrne in *Bullying: A Community Approach*.[1] It builds on the natural helping skills of children. It involves assigning selected student volunteers to 'be with' or 'befriend' peers whom teachers believe would benefit from peer support, such as new students or students who are shy and socially reticent. Befriending or being the buddy can involve purely practical help and informal chats, such as offering companionship and activities to those bullied or alone in the playground or in after school clubs, but it can also extend to 'buddy systems'.

A buddy system allows a bullied student to be befriended by another student of the same age with the aim of increasing their feeling of belonging. For 'befrienders' to be effective, training may be necessary to develop the skills of active listening, assertiveness and leadership.

Studies of befriending show many positives not only for the befriended, but also for the befrienders. Helen Cowie and Jennifer

Dawn report in VISTA[2] that the befrienders gain in confidence and learn to value other people more. Also, teachers report that the school environment becomes increasingly safe and caring, and that overall peer relationships improve.

Circle of Friends

Circle of Friends, also known as Circles of Support, are aimed at providing strong emotional support to students who have been identified as isolated or rejected by their peers. Students are trained to befriend and support classmates identified as being at risk of victimisation. Importantly, the Circle of Friends can also be used to support students who, as a result of bullying others, have been isolated or rejected.

With the agreement of the victimised student, the class teacher, counsellor or educational psychologist first holds a class meeting without the bullied child present. The facilitator encourages the whole class to give a positive picture of the child before they start airing what they find difficult about the student in question. They are also asked to consider how they would feel if they were in his/her shoes and, finally, to consider how they might help to improve the level of acceptance and inclusion of the student. The facilitator then invites a group of six to eight volunteers to make up the Circle of Friends. The Circle of Friends then sit down with the student in question to clarify how they intend to help them make friends and change any negative behaviour that may mitigate against that.

Circle of Friends has proved to be a very flexible and creative method to form positive relationships with peers.[3] Although the UK anti-bullying pack, *Bullying: Don't Suffer in Silence*, stresses that training is essential, I believe there is scope to adopt it in a way which allows the whole class to be made up of circles of friends. A rota can then be set up for these circles to be on duty, so to speak, and look out for and befriend any student in their class who appears isolated or excluded until the problem is resolved. In order to promote optimal positive inter-pupil relationships within the whole class, these circles should change every so often.

School Watch

School Watch is a student-organised initiative developed by South Wales Police. When the UK anti-bullying pack went into production in 2003, School Watch was in operation in over one hundred primary schools in South Wales. A key objective of the method is to prevent bullying, racism and other forms of anti-social behaviour. A similar programme has been in operation in schools in Queensland to reduce vandalism, theft and arson. In these schools, the catch phrase of School Watch is 'Look, Listen, Report'.

While I am not aware of the method being used in Ireland, I believe it has much to offer schools that wish, in particular, to establish a good working relationship with Garda Juvenile Liaison Officers. According to the UK Department of Education and Skills, the method 'allows pupils to improve their environment by taking responsibility for their behaviour and their actions'. Bullying declines and children feel happier and more valued, and this is attributed in part to a sense of ownership that the children develop to the scheme.

The way the approach works is that the students select a management committee supported by the police and a designated member of staff. They then implement activities, such as a 'bully box', to report incidents. They also organise 'playground patrols', a 'friendship garden', conservation areas and community projects. In addition, neighbouring schools exchange ideas and promote friendships. The scheme benefits students both in terms of their personal and social development and, importantly, in their attitudes to the police. In effect, the students become more socially aware and responsible.[4]

Peer Mediation and Conflict Resolution

Peer mediation is a structured process in which students help to resolve conflicts among their peers. Mediation is a negotiation-based strategy. It is not about affording blame but, similar to other restorative approaches, it is about finding a win-win solution to an ongoing conflict. It is particularly suited to disputes resulting from jealousies, rumours, misunderstandings, bias-related bullying incidents (racism, sexism, homophobia and other forms of prejudice), fights, theft and destruction of personal property. More serious incidents and assaults would call for adult intervention.

A typical example of peer mediation would be the following, as given by Hendry and Mellor in their handbook on *Peer Support in Schools*:[5]

> Louise and Angie used to be 'best friends' but recent changes in the class, and an argument out of school, have left Louise feeling that she is being shunned and gossiped about by Angie. Louise approaches a peer mediator who listens to her concern and explains the mediator's role. The mediator then approaches Angie who agrees to use the service. The two girls meet with two peer mediators who listen to their points of view, help them to consider the impact of each other's behaviour and ask them to identify possible changes they can each make so that they will both be happier. This takes the form of an agreement that the mediators can follow up on at a later agreed time.

Mediation, as the above example illustrates, allows the disputants to:

- Define the problem. The disputants take it in turn to tell their story without interruption. The mediator clarifies issues that may not be too clear and then summarises what has been said.
- Identify and express their feelings and needs. The mediator once more clarifies and summarises what has been said.
- Hear the feelings and needs of the other person.
- Acknowledge each other's point of view.
- Brainstorm possible solutions. The mediator can write these down and allow each disputant time to consider the implications of each option for themselves and each other.
- Agree a course of action. The agreed solution is written down and signed by both disputants.
- Evaluate progress and repeat if necessary.

Students who learn to mediate develop skills of affirmation, co-operation, communication and negotiation. Normal practice is for schools to seek volunteers and then select for training those who they feel are most suitable. While I am aware that not all students in a class or year group wish to act as mediators, I believe that all students would benefit from being taught the skills of mediation before any attempt is made to select students to become mediators. The reason for this is that students who have been taught the skills of mediation will view conflict differently. Most importantly, it becomes education for living. Children who are taught to resolve conflict at a young age will not only be better able to cope with it throughout life, but will also have learned important interpersonal skills such as active listening, affirmation, co-operation, emotional literacy, impulse control, assertiveness and leadership. See Information Box below for skills needed to resolve conflict.

Information Box: How to Resolve Conflict

Communication
- Listen without interrupting.
- Show understanding of the problem.
- Present your point of view.
- Explain how you feel.

Negotiation
- Brainstorm possible solutions.
- Accept the need for compromise.
- Choose the fairest solution.
- Implement your plan.

Consolidation
- Evaluate your plan.
- Communicate your feelings.

The school curriculum (SPHE, CSPE, Religion, English) or, indeed, Circle Time can be used very effectively to lay the foundation stones for developing the skills and concepts that enable children of all ages to develop a non-violent, creative approach to conflict.

Rehearsing speaking and listening skills, taking turns and controlling impulses can start as early as the junior infant years. From age seven children are regarded as being able to take the perspectives of others.[6]

How Effective is Peer Mediation?

I undertook an evaluation of a peer mediation programme as part of a European project, 'Gesposit'.[7] The peer mediation programme began small, with all first-year post-primary students and one third-year class in St Andrew's College, Dublin, being taught the skills necessary for conflict resolution and mediation as part of their religion classes. The students who volunteered at the completion of the training to act as mediators at first started to mediate in the junior school. When they gained in experience, confidence and age, the mediation extended up through the other years in the school. It can be seen that it is now school policy that all first-year students receive training in conflict resolution and mediation, irrespective of whether or not the students wish to join the rota of mediators.[8]

At the end of its first year of operation, I found the results to be very encouraging, particularly among the older students whose form teacher was the one who delivered the training programme. Among the older students there was a reduction in victimisation of 30 per cent, with no student reporting frequent victimisation. I also found that students who had acted as mediators were more effective at resolving arguments that they themselves had than were those who merely participated in the training programme.

Ellis Hennessy, in her review article on the 'The Value of Peer Mediation in School: A Review and Evaluation of Research Evidence',[9] notes that studies that have been published have generally not looked at the extent to which the mediators are able to transfer their skills outside of the school context. However, I am happy to say that the results from St Andrew's College showed that 25 per cent of the first-year students and over 52 per cent (66.7 per cent girls and 38.5 per cent boys) of the third-year students found the mediation training programme helped them to deal with conflicts that they had at home. Two-thirds of those whom it most benefited were again those who had acted as mediators. Parents' views were also sought and nearly half (46 per cent) reported that mediation had helped their child to deal with disagreements that arose between peers in the school. Over a quarter of parents (28.6 per cent) also felt that the training had helped their children to handle disagreements that they had with their teachers, a finding which was confirmed by the students themselves.[10]

When parents were asked how they felt the programme had helped their children, they reported the main benefits to be:

- an increase in confidence and maturity;
- a more open attitude to others' points of view;
- an increased awareness of other people's problems;
- a better communication style;
- an awareness of varying methods of dealing with everyday problems and disputes both at home and at school.

There were also lessons to be learned that support other studies, one being that more girls than boys volunteered to be mediators. This clearly benefited the girls, although teachers had noted a significant reduction of physical bullying among the boys. However, clearly ways need to be sought to motivate more boys to act as mediators, as it will help to strengthen their skills of conflict resolution and mediation beyond that which is gained by simply participating in the training sessions. Another lesson was that teachers must keep up the same degree of vigilance and level of intervention after the introduction of mediation as before it. Namely, students perceived their teachers as less committed to stopping bullying once the students had learned the skills to do so themselves. Whereas the teachers may have held back from intervening to give the students a better chance to practise their newfound skills, evidence is very clear that peer mediation works best when a climate of non-acceptance of bullying is generated by all members of the school community. Lack of teacher intervention can all too easily undermine such a climate, sending instead messages to students that are paramount to acceptance of aggression and bullying. This may go some way to explain why Farrington and Ttofi did not find formal engagement of peers in tackling bullying to decrease the level of victimisation.[11]

Other evaluation studies of peer mediation have shown that in addition to making the school climate more positive and reducing students' perception of the level of bullying, it is associated with drops in suspension and expulsions.[12] Thus, with adequate attention to details of planning, training and ongoing monitoring, there is little doubt that peer mediation is a promising tool for both primary and post-primary schools to help schools prevent and counter conflict and bullying.

Counselling

Of all restorative approaches to prevent and counter bullying, peer counselling is probably the one that requires the most training, maturity and expertise on the part of students. Although the skills needed are similar to peer mediation, peer counselling also requires regular supervision by teachers with a background in or good understanding of counselling, or by qualified counsellors on the staff.

Typically, students are first nominated by their peers or teachers and then interviewed for suitability before being selected for training. Students train through role plays, discussion and supervision, most often conducted by qualified counsellors or educational psychologists.

Peer counselling has the potential to help students who feel hurt and distressed to release or discharge their emotions in a safe and trusting environment. It provides particularly a valuable outlet for students who do not wish to share their concerns with their parents or teachers; knowing that they can speak openly and that the discussions are private really helps. While most peer counselling is conducted during lunch and break time, in some systems peer counselling operates a telephone helpline.

As with peer mediation, peer counselling has more difficulty recruiting boys than girls and their drop-out rate is also higher because of peer pressure. There is also some evidence that peer supporters are at risk of adverse comments, jealousy and loss of friendships. In addition, where levels of bullying are high, counselling-based approaches may find it difficult to challenge the culture of bullying. However, where the programmes are firmly embedded and are part of a broader schoolwide anti-bullying programme, the whole culture and climate in schools has been found to improve and victims of bullying find it easier to tell another person.

Peer Mentoring

Peer mentoring usually involves a one-to-one relationship between a younger student (mentee) and a more senior student (mentor). However, as Hendry and Mellor[13] point out, a vulnerable student may also meet with two older students together with three of his/her peers once a week during lunchtime and again after school. The time might be given over to structured games, help with homework and general opportunities to talk more freely about feelings and personal difficulties. The mentors act as role models providing reassurance and support and, where appropriate, offering advice. The advice might be how to prevent getting into fights, how to resolve disputes or how to more easily make friends. Mentors will also be trained to refer students on when there is a need for help beyond what they feel they can provide themselves.

Peer Support and the Internet (Cyber-Mentors)

All the above restorative approaches that I have so far described involve face-to-face support. Now that students are increasingly involved in electronic communication, it stands to reason that schools should work towards providing online peer support. This would also serve the need of students who are more comfortable talking to people online than in person. A school could, for example, have cyber-mentors who at lunchtime, break time or after school offer active listening and practical advice to peers, who for one reason or the other are feeling low or may be experiencing bullying or cyber-bullying. As with the Beat Bullying website on cyber-mentors,[14] individual schools can develop a dedicated website that allows students to send a message to or talk to a cyber-mentor in the chat room. The site will naturally need to be secure so that all chats are private. Should serious problems arise, the cyber-mentors will, as is generally the case with all peer supporters, refer the student to a staff member, qualified counsellor or psychologist on the staff.

Key Messages

- Peer support strategies give students the confidence to intervene when they witness bullying incidents.
- Peer support strategies promote a collective sense of responsibility to prevent and counter bullying.
- Befriending/buddying provides great protection against victimisation.
- A 'Circle of Friends' gives strong emotional support to victims who are excluded by their peers.
- School Watch, similar to Neighbourhood Watch, empowers students to report bullying and to behave in a responsible manner.
- Peer mediation teaches students how to deal with and resolve conflict. It is a tool for life.

- Peer counselling strengthens skills of listening and responding to emotions. It also helps students find their own solutions.
- Cyber-mentors provide advice and guidance to students who are more comfortable communicating online than face-to-face.

Notes

1. Byrne, B., *Bullying: A Communtiy Approach*, Dublin: Columba Press, 1996.
2. *School Bullying and Violence: Taking Action*: www.vistop.org/ebook.
3. For a step-by-step guide to the strategy, see Newton, C. and Wilson, D., *Creating Circles of Friends: A Peer Support and Inclusion Workbook*, Nottingham: Inclusion Solutions, 2003.
4. Examples of the type of work that schools have undertaken within the scheme can be found in an article by George Ball, 'Promoting School Awareness and Responsibility in Primary School: The School Watch' in *Pastoral Care in Education: An International Journal of Personal, Social and Emotional Development*, 16.1 (1998), pp. 17–20.
5. Hendry, R. and Mellor, A., *Peer Support in Schools: A Handbook to Aid Development of Peer Support Systems in Primary, Secondary and Special Schools*, Edinburgh: The Anti-Bullying Network, 2005.
6. For details on how to introduce the skills of mediation to any age group, see *Let's Mediate* by Hilary Stacey and Pat Robinson (1997). Other great resources for primary school teachers are the S.A.L.T. Programme (Creative Solutions to Conflict), written by Fiona McAuslan (2008), and *Peer Mediation in Primary Schools* by Jerry Tyrrell and Seamus Farrell from the Centre for the Study of Conflict at the University of Ulster. In addition, teachers can see peer mediation in practice by logging on as a guest to the Parents Pathway on Vistop (www.vistop.org).
7. Gesposit (PO-001) European Commission Education & Culture Connect Initiative, (DG XXII): *Combating Violence in Schools*, proceedings of Conferência Internacional Prevencão da Violência na Escola, Lisbon, University Alberta, 26–27 December 2002.
8. Godsil, A., *Peer Mediation and its Potential for Reducing the Incidence of Bullying in Schools*, proceedings of the Second National Conference on Bullying and Suicide in Schools, organised by the Irish Association of Suicidology and the National Suicide Review Group, held in Tralee, 28–29 November 2002.
9. Hennessy, E., 'The Value of Peer Mediation in Schools: A Review and Evaluation of Research Evidence', *Irish Psychologist*, 35 (2008), p. 20–23.
10. O'Moore, M. and McGuire, L., T*he Effectiveness of Peer Mediation to Resolve Conflict and Violence in School*, Gesposit: EU Connect PT-001 and the Anti-Bullying Centre, Trinity College Dublin.
11. Farrington, D.P. and Ttofi, M.M., *School-Based Programmes to Reduce Bullying and Victimisation*, Campbell Systematic Reviews, Oslo: The Campbell Collaboration, 2009.
12. Ibid.
13. Hendry and Mellor (2005), op. cit.
14. www.cybermentors.org.uk.

PART THREE

13 WHAT PARENTS CAN DO TO COUNTER BULLYING

Steps Parents Can Take to Prevent Victimisation and Bullying

Clearly no child or teenager deserves to be bullied, even though, on occasion, they may have wrong on their side. To be bullied is a most terrifying and upsetting experience. In the face of a hammer blow to their confidence and self-esteem, it can render victims feeling worthless, unhappy and powerless so that they perceive life to offer them little or no future. I have explored the powerful emotions associated with victimisation, but the following excerpt by Elaine Doyle, taken from the *Proceedings of the Second National Conference on Bullying and Suicide in Schools*,[1] gives some insight into the trauma that can push some young people to consider or complete suicide as a result of bullying. Elaine Doyle had loving parents. She was attractive and intelligent, but she came under the spotlight because she achieved 100 per cent in a physics test, a success which sparked unstoppable jealousy from some of her peers. This is what Elaine Doyle, who so often thought of ending her life, told the conference:

> Words cannot possibly describe the feelings that I suffered – isolation, rejection, insecurity, depression, the list goes on. I think the isolation hurt the most, had the biggest, most harmful effect. I felt so alone, so afraid like as if I was trapped in a nightmare I just couldn't get out of. I didn't feel safe anywhere, not even at home because no matter where I was there was so much going on in my head I could never escape the torture. I could stand here for hours and describe all the feelings but you couldn't even begin to understand how tough it actually was. My family watched me suffer for months and they do understand how hard it was, but only to a certain extent.[2]

Elaine also had this to say:

> My self-esteem and confidence had been destroyed. I became extremely paranoid and pessimistic. I felt I was the only person that this had ever happened to; I didn't see a way out. I felt that nobody understood what I was going through. I spent a lot of time at home, rarely left the house. I stopped taking care of myself: my health was at an all time low.[3]

Any parent or guardian reading this who has experienced their child or teenager being bullied will recognise these symptoms. It is only reasonable to expect that every responsible parent is concerned for the protection, safety and well-being of his or her child. Thus, to find out that one's child or teenager is being bullied is sure to bring forth a mix of emotions. Many a parent has told me that they have experienced shock, heightened anger, frustration, feelings of wanting revenge, upset and guilt on learning of their child's victimisation.

Guilt is particularly heightened and often difficult to come to terms with when a parent or guardian has overlooked the signs and symptoms of bullying and, as a result, has come to realise that they failed to identify any changes of behaviour that they may have noticed as bullying. Parents of teenagers, for example, can so easily put mood changes down to the normal stresses and strains of adolescence. Parents may also feel guilty that they have failed their child by not having instilled in them what they may see as greater resilience or skills to counteract bullying. Worse still are the feelings of guilt that are experienced should they discover that they have been punishing their child for behaviours that were in effect the result of bullying (see p. 52 for signs and symptoms of bullying).

No parent should feel guilty or torture themselves if they have missed out or been slow to recognise bullying, as it can be exceedingly difficult to be certain that bullying is the problem. Many a parent will have found themselves none the wiser after questioning their bullied child or teenager about concerns around bullying, as young people can be most adept at fobbing adults off with what may appear to be plausible excuses. Take Elaine Doyle, for example, the former victim I referred to earlier. She reported how on one occasion when she watched TV with her mum about bullying, she turned to her and said, 'How can people let that happen to them and not say anything to anyone? I know I wouldn't be able to suffer in silence.' Yet Elaine found that 'when you are in the situation yourself, all common sense goes out the window'.

In spite of the fact that Elaine belonged to a family that was very close and very open, so much so that they talked to each other about everything, she did not tell them about her bullying before months had passed. Unsure of why that was, she confirmed what so many victims, both young and old, tell me: 'I think it was a mixture of being ashamed, not wanting to admit it, not fully understanding what actually happened. I hated people referring to it as bullying and any time my parents were talking about it, I'd correct them and say, "I got a bit of hassle".'

The *Diary of Leanne Wolfe*,[4] a copy of which all schools may now have in their possession to raise awareness, is further evidence of just how adept victims of bullying can be at hiding the fact that they are being bullied.

Become Informed

Bearing in mind the high incidence of bullying in our schools and how reluctant children and teenagers are to let parents know about it, the best any parent can do for their child is to first become acquainted with the signs and symptoms of being a victim of bullying and of bullying others, as detailed in Chapters 2 and 4. In this way they can make as early an intervention as possible and, thus, prevent the more serious ill effects of ongoing victimisation and bullying of others (see Chapter 5). Secondly, parents need to become acquainted with interventions that have proved to be effective in stopping bullying.

Before advising any reader what they can do should they find out their child is being bullied, is bullying others or both, I would first like to dwell on what all parents can do to prevent bullying. In helping to prevent bullying, the chances of a child becoming a victim, a bully or both will be greatly reduced.

Steps to Prevention

1. Talk to Your Child About Bullying and Cyber-Bullying

It is critical that children grow up in a home where inappropriate aggression and bullying is condemned and the stigma associated with victimisation is put to bed. Remember, if there were no 'bullies' we would have no victims. Thus, the onus that is often placed on victims to change their response or behaviour either by becoming more assertive, less sensitive or by ignoring what is said or done needs to be challenged. It is not unusual for parents to hear teachers or principals respond to their complaints of bullying by suggesting that their child needs to toughen up and learn to take the knocks that come with going to school. Yet none of the traits that may have predisposed their child to victimisation, such as sensitivity, anxiety or a passive nature, were a threat to the health, safety and well-being of others. On the other hand, the behavioural traits of children who bully, which clearly are a threat and cost to society, are all too often condoned. It is, therefore, imperative that every adult takes responsibility for condemning behaviour that deliberately sets out to cause harm to others. This can be best achieved by correcting all inappropriate aggression and leading by example.

In view of the fact that it will take time for there to be a significant shift in society's attitude to bullying, any parent reading this should take the precaution of making their child aware of the fact that anyone at any stage in their life can be targeted, and should it happen to them, whether in or out of school, they must not feel that they are at fault. Instead, the message to get across to your child is that the problem lies with the bully, that he or she has some unresolved personal or emotional issues. The more a child is able to understand and attribute the hurtful and cowardly actions of bullying to the bully's own inadequate personality, the less damage will be caused to their self-esteem.

Equally, the more a child grows up with learning about the wrongs of bullying because of the hurt it causes, the greater the chance will be that they will refrain from bullying others and the more open they will become to changing their behaviour.

Plant ideas of ways to respond to being targeted. Let the child know that in the event of being targeted there are some things they can do to prevent further attacks. It would be well worth the effort to practise or do role play to demonstrate some of the responses that are recognised as being effective in stopping bullying. By being forewarned, children will be forearmed.

For traditional bullying tactics, the main response options are as follows:

- Act confident. Stand up straight, catch the bully's eyes and in a firm and clear voice tell them to stop or else you will report their behaviour to a teacher. Remembering that the bully is the one with the problem, a good assertive response can also be, 'What's your problem?' Also effective is to say in a loud voice so that others can hear, 'Stop bullying me' or, 'You are nothing but a bully'. The 'bully' does not like to be shown up or lose face.
- Use humour. Using humour can help to diffuse the tactics of a 'bully'. Humour denies the 'bully' the upset reaction they seek and on which they thrive. So practise or role play witty responses. For example, if the bully says, 'You're dumb', the child can say, 'Well, that makes two of us', 'Thanks for telling me the truth' or simply, 'Yeah, thanks for that', 'Cheers' or, 'Have you looked at yourself in the mirror at all?'
- Laugh it off or say nothing. Don't let them see you are bothered by teasing, slagging or name-calling. Either laugh it off, shrugging the shoulders, or make no reply at all. Pretend you didn't hear them or it didn't bother you.
- Use 'fogging'. Pretend you are wrapped in a fog. You can't hear or see the bully or his/her followers. Say to yourself, 'What a sad bunch' or, 'Losers' and, 'No matter what anyone says or does to me I am a worthwhile person'.
- Don't hit out or physically fight. As tempting as this may be, if the bully should lose out, he or she can so easily seek revenge by getting a gang together and then launch a vicious physical attack on the child. This could lead to serious injuries or even a fatality.

For cyber-bullying, the main options are as follows:

- Don't reply
- Save the message, film clip or the full screen content

- Block the sender
- Tell a trusted friend, parent or teacher
- Consider reporting the offensive material to the appropriate service provider.

2. It's Okay to Tell

Another critical message to get across to children is that it is natural to feel scared, upset and even helpless when people get at you time and time again. Tell them that if they feel like this and they can't get the bully to stop in spite of trying, the correct thing to do is to let someone know. In that way they are acting responsibly because it allows an adult, such as a teacher, to correct the problematic behaviour of the 'bully'. By not reporting the problem, on the other hand, they should know that they are adding to the 'bully's' power, as silence becomes their best friend. The message from parents should be, 'If you need help, let me know' or, 'If you need help, go to your teacher'. There should be no shame attached to telling. Telling is acting responsibly.

There are now many good books for various age groups that are beautifully illustrated and can help parents to give their children a very good understanding of bullying, for example, *Resolving Bullying* (for ages six–twelve) by Fiona McAuslan and Peter Nicholson (Veritas, 2010) and *Bye-Bye, Bully! A Kid's Guide for Dealing with Bullies'* (for age four upwards) by J.S. Jackson and illustrated by R.W. Alley (Abbey Press, Indiana, 2003). Teenagers can be directed to self-help books such as *Don't Pick on Me* by Rosemary Stones (Piccadilly Press, 1993) and 'What All Young People Need to Know', a chapter in *Dealing with Bullying in Schools* by Stephen Minton and myself (Paul Chapman, 2004). Also not to be underestimated is *101 Ways to Deal with Bullying* by Michele Elliot of the children's charity, Kidscape, in the UK.

3. Talk to Your Child about Peer Pressure

In the same way that you should talk and prepare your child for bullying, so should you talk to them about peer pressure, because it can cause your child to become involved in bullying. Every child and teenager wants to have friends, to belong to a group and to be respected and feel valued as a member of a group. Indeed, the only reason some children say they put up with school is because they want to be with friends. As children become teenagers, the peer group becomes ever more important to them. Becoming more independent from their parents and in their search for status, independence, achievement and a satisfying philosophy of life, they seek to spend ever more time with their peers. They find them a source of immense social support and identity.

It is not uncommon for conflict to arise between parents and their teenagers if they are associating with friends or peers whom they feel do not share the same values as they do. While most teenagers manage to find the space and freedom to grow up with like-minded friends, there is no doubt that some fall prey to peer pressure that is alien to the way in which they have been brought up.

There is no better example of the negative forces of belonging to a group and the peer pressure that follows than to reflect on the tragic case of Brian Murphy, who died outside of the Burlington Hotel. Whatever values the group held as individuals due to their parenting and education became diffused and, as a result, they collectively demonstrated an inability to control their aggressive impulses and discern right from wrong. Temporarily, mob rule took over.

The significance of peer groups is also strongly reflected by an account given by Brendan Byrne of a fourteen-year-old girl who stated: 'You try to steer clear of the bullies. But when you are in the group you don't have a say in it if they are bullying. You don't want to be bullied, so you try to act like a bully or you will be kicked out.'[5] Children need to hear it from adults that they do not have to be everybody's friend. Not everyone is going to like them, but that is to be expected and it is perfectly normal, the adult world being no different. They should also be told that they do not need to be perfect. It takes all types to make a world and it is not possible to know for sure what perfect is. Everyone has different tastes, so what may be perfect to one person is not to another.

The attributes that prevent children and teenagers from becoming involved in aggression and violence are:

- A resilient temperament
- A warm and affectionate relationship with at least one parent

- Parents who provide affectionate supervision
- Parents who have pro-social beliefs
- Parents who exercise consistent discipline
- Parents who display a strong interest in their child and friends.

To prepare your child or teenager as much as possible to resist the negative forces of peer pressure requires that you instil in them a strong sense of what is right and what is wrong. Everyone knows what makes for a fair and just society. As a parent, the challenge lies in leading by example and correcting behaviour that is clearly disrespectful and harmful. A strong sense of self-worth and identity is also a critical factor in avoiding what is known to be morally wrong. With inner strength, children and teenagers do not need:

- to be someone they are not;
- to behave like someone else;
- to dress like someone else.

Instead, they can be themselves and be proud for standing up for what they are. Remember, it is the children with high self-esteem who are least likely to become involved in bullying, either as a bully, a victim or both, and the most willing to intervene and defend a victim.

4. Building Assertiveness Skills

There are three response styles common to children and adults:

- Passive
- Aggressive/hostile
- Assertive.

Assertive people tend to stand up for themselves without being aggressive or violent. Children and teenagers who are comfortably assertive will maintain good eye contact, stand tall and use a clear and steady voice to express what they want or how they feel about things. With such attributes they are in a better position to shake off a 'bully' and also to avoid aggression, such as physical fighting or engaging in a verbal 'slagging match' to settle their differences. Passive children, on the other hand, are inclined not to take action and instead suffer in silence, therefore it is easy to see how they are prone to being picked on. Aggressive children, in contrast to both passive and assertive children, will have scant regard for other people's rights or feelings as long as they can satisfy their own.

There is no better way to build assertiveness in your child than for them to witness assertiveness in the home on a daily basis. This means that as parents one needs to be direct and straightforward when communicating with each other and one's children. It is expected, of course, that a degree of sensitivity should also be displayed, as account should always be taken of when it might be most appropriate to state what needs to be said. Learning to use 'I' statements is the secret of good assertive communication. For example, 'I don't agree with you' is preferable to saying, 'You are talking rubbish' and, 'I want you to stop taking my things' is better than saying, 'You're nothing but a thief'.

Good assertive skills also involve being willing to listen so that judgement is suspended until such time as others have been heard and understood. A critical aspect of assertiveness is mutual respect and this is reflected by listening and then responding in a firm, respectful manner. Remaining calm and in control is yet another assertive skill, so every effort should be made to avoid reactive responses that are emotional, impulsive and angry. Later on I will detail how you can teach your child to relax and manage anger should that be a problem your child may be experiencing.

Most importantly, assertiveness builds a child's self-esteem, because when children find that they can handle conflicts and express their needs in a satisfactory manner they will feel good. This contrasts with the more common feelings of frustration, self-criticism and even anger when arguments are lost or when no opinions are offered at all out of fear.

5. Build Empathy

In the words of Professor Marin Hoffman of New York University, 'Empathy is the spark of human concern for others, the glue that makes social life possible'.[6] Empathy, therefore, plays a key role in the prevention of aggression and bullying. When we talk about children who lack empathy, we generally mean children who show little regard or concern for the feelings of others. This is not to say that they do not understand how people feel when they are hurt, but rather that they don't care about their feelings. Children who bully understand only too well the feelings of hurt at being abused, having most probably experienced aggressive outbursts themselves at home or in school. We refer to this understanding as cognitive empathy. Unless children with cognitive empathy also reflect affective or emotional empathy, which is consideration for others, they have the perfect weapon to hurt others because they know all the soft spots.

It is, therefore, critical that children develop affective empathy, that of showing consideration for others so that they do not do to others what they would not like done to themselves. This can best be achieved if parents actively socialise their child to consider others, which is often referred to as 'caring morality'. Thus, whenever as parents you are a witness to acts of inappropriate aggression by your child, try to provide corrective feedback in a way that puts pressure on your child to control his/her behaviour, while at the same time having your child consider the needs and claims of the other person. By encouraging your child to talk about his/her feelings about wrongdoing, as well as consider the opponent's feelings (for example, 'What do you think Johnny thinks when you kick him?'), you are developing empathy as well as sowing the seeds of emotional literacy and mutual respect. When children are emotionally literate they are better able to understand, express and cope with emotions in an appropriate way. The ability to understand oneself and others, especially another person's perspective, lays the foundation for morally responsible behaviour and good conflict resolution skills.

Mary Gordon, the author of *Roots of Empathy*, is careful to point out that emotional literacy can only develop in an environment where children feel safe and supported. She stresses that when children 'feel criticised, ridiculed or not respected, they are at risk of shutting down any expression of emotion'. Their feelings instead will go underground and, as communication becomes thwarted, the child does not learn to seek solutions to the emotions that were felt.[7]

Consider, for example, a child coming home admitting to some anti-social act that he/she committed in school and then being severely criticised for it before being given the opportunity to express the feelings that prompted the behaviour. With such an outcome the chances are that the child will not only learn to avoid telling parents of any future wrongdoing, but also a great opportunity will have been missed to help the child gain:

- a greater understanding of their emotions;
- the cause of their emotions;
- a better way of controlling their emotions.

It is important, therefore, for parents when dealing with a child that has hurt or bullied another to start by asking their child how they felt at the time. This can be prompted by the parent saying something like, 'Oh, you must have felt very angry'. By taking every opportunity to help your child to become more competent in understanding their own feelings and those of others you will help them to prevent and deal with conflicts more effectively.

6. Building Self-Esteem

A child with high self-esteem is a happy and resourceful child and is less likely to be a victim of long-term bullying or to become involved in bullying behaviour. In one of my studies I found that 50 per cent of children who bullied hated school and 46 per cent said they were often sad. No one is born with negative feelings about themselves. Children who feel negative or bad about themselves have received the message that somehow they are unlovable and not worth much.

As a parent you are in the best position to give your child the gift of acceptance. Give them plenty of experiences and take every opportunity to play to their strengths. Frequently praise, reward and recognise your child's efforts and unique qualities. The positive parental voices will become internalised and will help to nurture your child's self-esteem. Also give your child responsibility; seek their help on opinions and issues. This helps to let them know that you value them and that you have confidence in their resourcefulness. In addition, it helps to give them a sense of belonging and a positive sense of their capability.

Parents will recognise that they may say things to their child that they later regret, especially when they are stressed. It is important, therefore, to try not to vent one's emotions and say something to or about your child that is destructively critical, derogatory or belittling. Equally discourage your child from saying anything negative or destructively critical about him/herself. Help them raise their sights and to focus on their strengths.

A Special Note

You may have come across differing opinions about praise, saying that too much praise can be a bad thing because it can give a child a false sense of confidence, which can leave them unprepared for failure and disappointments as they face the challenges of school life. However, this is only the case when praise is used totally indiscriminately instead of using it to recognise genuine effort and achievement.

7. Build Resilience

Resilience is very much tied in with a sturdy sense of self and one's worth. Children and teenagers who are resilient are better able to take criticism and deal with disappointments in a cool and calm manner. They will bounce back and learn from the negative experience. Because they are comfortable with who they are, they also have no difficulty seeking help when it is needed. Irrespective of intelligence or learning difficulties, they recognise their strengths and use them. They are not discouraged or ashamed by their deficits because they are aware of their capabilities and strengths. Indeed, they would undoubtedly share the American humorist Will Roger's sentiment that, 'Everybody is ignorant, only on different subjects'.

Children low on resilience, on the other hand, tend to take difficulties and criticisms personally, prompting feelings of inadequacy and pessimism. This, in turn, can trigger coping strategies that are counterproductive or self-defeating. Instead of bouncing back in a positive manner, the self-defeating strategies may lead to avoiding, attention-seeking or aggressive behaviour, such as clowning, bullying and even quitting or dropping out.

To help your child develop high resilience, take every opportunity to develop:

- Independence. Give your child tasks to do on their own, like jobs in the house or garden.
- Focus on effort rather than the ultimate result. Help them learn from mistakes and develop a sense of mastery.
- Interpersonal skills. Allow your child to express his/herself freely. Also encourage them to listen and see things from the other person's perspective. This helps also to promote empathy and assertiveness.
- Self-control. Let your child participate in as many activities as possible without undue adult interference and control. In this way they will gain confidence in handling diverse situations on their own.
- Avoid criticism and punishments. Instead, take a restorative approach and help your child to take responsibility for wrongdoing and to make amends. Criticism that is too severe will lead to denial and placing blame on others.
- Being comfortable with who they are. Radiate unconditional love. Be accepting and give them the sense that you enjoy their company. Do not set the bar too high so that your child feels under undue pressure to live up to your expectations of their academic performance or behaviour, as this can so easily lead to a sense of failure. Instead, accept and treasure your child for his/her uniqueness.

8. Encourage Friendships

Having quality friends will help to protect your child from being picked on and rejected by their peer group. It will also prevent your child from belonging to peer groups or cliques that place pressure on their members to behave in a manner that is anti-social or hurtful to others. The way to encourage good friendships is to be accepting and positive of them when they are around your child. Encourage your child to have his/her school friends home. Create something special from time to time, like an outing that is fun, adventurous and displays generosity. All of this will strengthen the bond between your child and his/her friends. Also helpful is to become acquainted with the parents of your child's friends as they can be a great source of information should you sense that your child is being bullied.

Make sure your child understands that good friendships are built on respect, loyalty, kindness, honesty and empathy. It is critical that parents model these behaviours when meeting and talking with or about their own circle of friends.

9. Encourage Sport

Sport has so many positive attributes that helps to build a well-adjusted child, both socially and emotionally. Sport has the ability to transcend religion, race and politics and allows children to be physically active while at the same time have fun, play by the rules and, importantly, make friends. With sport children build confidence. They learn the value of teamwork and how to accept winning and losing as part of the game. They will discover the value of their own contribution in the effort that they put into the game to help secure success.

Above all else, sport provides an excellent opportunity for children to learn the principles of fair play, which is real education for living. The European Sports Charter and Code of Ethics by the Council of Europe (1993) defines fair play as 'much more than playing within the rules. It incorporates the concepts of friendship, respect for others and always playing within the right spirit. Fair play is defined as a way of thinking, not just a way of behaving. It incorporates issues concerned with the elimination of cheating, gamesmanship, doping, violence (both physical and verbal), exploitation, unequal opportunities, excessive commercialisation and corruption.'[8]

Most parents will have witnessed that when the chips are down and there is pressure on children to win games, not all of the above laudable aims are adhered to. Parents on the sidelines can often be the worst offenders. But we are beginning to see more consistent refereeing and penalties handed out for breaches in the rules. Parents who may be fearful of the competitive element of sport, and indeed the violence that is all too often associated with it, should be reassured by the Code of Ethics and Good Practice for Children's Sport, developed by the Irish Sports Council for Ireland and Northern Ireland, which will greatly benefit children, parents/guardians and sports leaders.[9] The purpose is to ensure that children have positive and enjoyable experiences while engaging with sport, irrespective of their ability, gender, social class or race.

A Special Note

While the value of sport cannot be overemphasised, no child should feel dispirited or a failure if they feel it is not for them. Other outlets should be sought. Alternatives such as Scouts and Guides, music, dance, drama and martial arts have the same capacity as sport to provide personal achievement and build confidence, self-esteem and self-discipline.

Martial arts can be especially valuable in empowering anxious and fearful children to feel more confident about handling potential aggressive acts that may be involved in bullying. Martial arts does not only provide children with the skills to better defend themselves, it also focuses on teaching children how to avoid physical confrontations. Indeed, good martial arts classes teach that fighting back physically is the last resort. A child who has displayed tendencies to become involved in bullying, either as a victim, bully or both, would benefit greatly from the confidence-building and self-discipline skills that are inherent in martial arts training.

10. Encourage Skills of Conflict Resolution and Mediation

If your child learns early to master the skills of mediation, dealing with conflict will become so much easier. They will be spared many of the emotions associated with unresolved conflicts, such as frustration, hostility, withdrawal, anger, unhappiness and poor self-esteem. In developing skills of mediation, children learn to:

- express their feelings;
- listen without interrupting;
- manage their anger;
- collaborate in finding a solution.

There is no better way for children to learn these skills than for parents to model them whenever there are disputes and disagreements in the home. Children will learn that collaboration and communication is at the heart of good conflict resolution. If the skills are consistently applied at home, they will become part of a child's behavioural toolbox, which can then be easily transferred to situations outside of the home and in school. If as parents you would like to see how easy children can take to mediating conflicts among themselves, you can log onto www.vistop.org as a guest and select the 'Parents Pathway', where you can view children engaging in peer mediation.

11. Encourage the Role of Defender

I am sure every parent would like to think of their child as someone who might offer some help or support to a fellow student whom they see is being bullied. Sadly, peer support is not a given within a school community, no more than it is in the workplace. Children, like adults, are clearly fearful of helping an injured party for fear of negative consequences to themselves. However, society can only hope to survive if everyone looks out for each other.

Being a defender ties in with empathy and self-esteem, and we know that children who show strong empathy and high self-esteem will be more inclined to defend a victim than a child who is low on these qualities. However, it is also about values. Children need to learn from their parents or guardians, and to have it reinforced by teachers, that to help someone when they are down and unable to defend themselves is to act responsibly and in the best interests of society. There is no shortage of examples of how individuals and society have benefited from the actions of courageous whistleblowers.

Below are some tips you can give your child to empower them as a witness to take action against bullying; bystander training has the ability to increase intervention in children and teenagers.

- Talk to the bully or bullies. Tell them to stop, otherwise you will report them to the teacher. Children should remember that most often as a bystander they are not alone, so together with their friends they are most likely to outnumber the bully. Therefore, they can well afford to take some positive action to stop the bullying. By not intervening they should understand that their behaviour will be interpreted as showing approval and support for the perpetrators.
- If unable to defend the victim, report the incident to a staff member.
- Share your 'bystander' feelings of anxiety, fear or anger with your family.

- Do not be manipulated by the distorted thinking of the perpetrator(s), for example, that the victim is deserving of the treatment or it's only a bit of fun.
- Never get caught joining in with onlookers and laughing at the victim when he/she is mistreated.
- Befriend the victim. Encourage them or assist them in reporting the bullying. Remember you will always be remembered by your peers for your behaviour in school.

A Special Note

All too often I meet with parents who, in recalling their school days, express feelings of shame and guilt for not having taken any positive action to help a fellow student who was cruelly victimised, especially when they knew that it contributed to them dropping out of school or suffering from social and emotional difficulties. If you as a parent can relate to this, then make sure that your child does not have to go through life with similar feelings. These feelings are clearly illustrated in our DVD, *Silent Witnesses*, designed to empower students to counter bullying. You can view it or ask your teenage son or daughter to view it by going to www.vistop.org, or seek a copy from Trinity College's Anti-Bullying Centre.

Thus, to prevent your children having unnecessary feelings of shame and guilt in respect of bullying, whether in the short term or long term, make sure to build and reinforce the attitude that it is wrong to bully or to assist or reinforce anyone else in doing so. Should they witness bullying, encourage them to take action, even if this means having to report it.

Key Messages

- Talk to your child about bullying. Make sure they understand why it is wrong to bully or to assist or reinforce any fellow student who might be bullying.
- Prepare your child for the possible event of being targeted or tested as a potential victim. The problem is generally not theirs but lies with the bully, who may be feeling insecure, frustrated and inferior in some way. Chat to them and even role play possible responses to stop any escalation of bullying.

- Talk to your child about peer pressure.
- Build assertiveness.
- Encourage good social skills, especially empathy.
- Develop good moral reasoning.
- Build confidence and positive self-esteem. Give them attention, love and approval.
- Build resilience.
- Encourage strong friendships.
- Encourage sport, hobbies and extra-curricular activities.
- Model and teach your child the skills of conflict resolution and mediation.
- Encourage your child to be a defender.

Notes

1. Doyle, E., 'Buying Time' in *Proceedings of the Second National Conference on Bullying and Suicide in Schools*, the Irish Association of Suicidology and the National Suicide Review Group, Castlebar, Mayo: *Connaught Telegraph*, 2002.
2. Ibid.
3. Ibid.
4. *The Diary of Leanne Wolfe*, RTÉ Radio 1: Documentary on One, 2008: www. rte. ie/radio1/doconone.
5. *Irish Times*, 6 February 1996.
6. Hoffman, M.L., *Empathy and Moral Development: Implications for Caring and Justice*, Cambridge: Cambridge University Press, 2000.
7. Gordon, M., *Roots of Empathy: Changing the World Child by Child*, New York: The Experiment, 2009.
8. *The European Sports Charter and Code of Ethics*, 1993, cited in *Code of Ethics & Good Practice for Children's Sport*, Irish Sports Council and the Sports Council for Northern Ireland, 2006.
9. Ibid.

14 STEPS TO TAKE IF YOUR CHILD IS BEING BULLIED

It can be very difficult, for reasons outlined in Chapter 2, to be certain that your child is being bullied. Children, and even more so teenagers, are notoriously reluctant to tell parents or teachers that they are being bullied. The reasons range from shame over perceived lack of popularity or inability to cope, guilt and fear of reprisals. However, the best guide is the intensity and duration of the tell-tale signs (see Chapter 2). When you notice that your child or teenager is out of sorts, especially from Monday to Friday, and is showing considerable reluctance in going to school and may even be feigning illness or, indeed, have genuine psychosomatic symptoms such as headaches, stomach cramps, nausea and vomiting, it is time to take action.

Start with gently trying to get your child to open up and unload the problem onto you. You can start by saying something to the effect of, 'I've noticed you're not yourself these days so I can't help wondering if someone is getting at you in school'. Explain that no one deserves to be bullied, but that it is a very common problem and that he/she is not alone in being bullied. Explain also that he/she should not feel any shame or guilt as those feelings should rightly belong to the perpetrators. Let your child know that if he/she has done nothing to provoke the bullying there is no reason why they should feel ashamed or guilty.

If you are met with a blanket stance of nothing being wrong (especially if they associate victimisation with failure), you may be able to help them save face by letting them know about famous people who have been bullied in their school days, for example, Tom Cruise, Mel Gibson, Gabriel Byrne and Sandra Bullock. Also, if you, your partner or any brothers or sisters you have were bullied, let them know because this helps to take the sting out of their predicament.

Victimisation will be seen as something that can happen to the best of people, people to whom they look up and admire. They will also get the chance to learn that it is a passing phase and that once a victim does not mean always a victim, but in order for it to stop some intervention will be needed.

Even if you get no confirmation from your child or teenager that he/she is being bullied, you can nonetheless proceed by giving them tips as to what is possible for them to do should they ever find themselves being bullied. You may, for example, get a self-help book, which you can say you got because of your concern about the damage that bullying can do. Gently and sympathetically proceed by going through some of the practical advice given as to how bullying can be stopped. If appropriate, offer the book to them so they can read it for themselves.

If there is no sign of improvement in mood and you are still left with a strong suspicion that your child is being bullied, you have two main choices. One is to go straight to the school and express your concerns and the other is to delay a little until you have some hard facts. If there is no one else in the family who knows anything, try to get in touch with the parents of your child's friends. They may be able to throw some light on your concerns or be able to find out something through their own children. Taking this latter course may give you the information you need to properly confront the issue with your child. It will also enable you to better make a decision as to whether to involve the school or not.

Involving the School

It should be noted that once the 'cat is out of the bag' and the bullying is exposed, it can act as a huge relief for your child. This, of course, will only be the case if they realise that you are not critical of them or think any less of them for being bullied. However, they may nonetheless plead with you not to let the school know because of their fear of what the bullies might do. You will need to reassure them that what you are doing is for the best and that you will not hide anything from them. Tell them that interventions that involve both parents and schools are more often than not successful. Even so, you need to be prepared for tantrums and aggressive outbursts, as they may not be able to let go of their fear of reprisals should the school become involved. However, you can be reassured that most often the very same children who cause the greatest fuss will soon show their appreciation once they realise that your intervention has had a positive effect and that it served to stop the bullying.

Before making contact with the school, find out if the school has laid down procedures for reporting incidents of bullying in their anti-bullying policy (it is mandatory that they have one). When speaking with the relevant staff member, it would be very helpful if you were to know the answers to the following questions:

- Who is involved?
- What form does the bullying take?
- Where does the bullying take place?
- When does it take place?
- How long has the bullying being going on?
- Were there any bystanders and who might they have been?

It is vital that when you give an account of events in person, over the phone or by e-mail that you try to remain non-critical and non-judgemental in order to prevent unnecessary defensive responses. Remember, the aim of the visit is to seek the school's help in stopping the bullying and this is better achieved if you take a no-blame approach. Give them the chance to investigate and report back to you, as laid out in their procedures.

Working With the School
In a similar manner to what schools are expected to do when they are dealing with reports of bullying, you should keep a record of the calls or meetings that you have with the school (the time of the meeting; with whom you met; what was agreed and when you will hear back from them). Depending on the age of your child, you can also encourage him/her to keep a diary, if they are not already doing so. Your child can get a lot of comfort from writing a diary about events and feelings they have experienced.

A log detailing the bullying incidents and a record of the school's actions are invaluable should it ever be necessary to take legal advice or issue proceedings, although I would recommend this course of action only as a last resort. If, as a parent, you should ever be tempted to take legal action due to lack of action or an obstructionist response from the school, get in touch first with the Anti-Bullying Centre, as they will be able to advise you as to whether there is anything else you might still be able to do before proceeding with a legal case.

As you liaise with the school, it is very important to keep your child informed of the progress that you make so that they are not caught off-guard by things that teachers or students who have been questioned about the bullying may say to them. Once you have gained the confidence of your child or teenager, you will find that they will be more inclined to unburden themselves to you in the event of any further episodes of bullying.

In your dealing with the school, staff may point to characteristics in your child that makes him/her an easy target of bullying. Do not take this as a criticism or that they are laying the blame on your child, rather, be open to the fact that what they say may be contributing to the victimisation. While it does not excuse the behaviour of the children bullying your child, it might point to valuable steps that you can take to help your child prevent being an easy target in the future. Social skills deficits, lack of assertiveness, impulsiveness or anxiety, for example, are all among the risk factors for being bullied (see Chapter 3), but all can be remedied with your help or the help of an external agency.

Dealing With the Most Common Forms of Bullying
Physical Bullying
If your son or daughter is being physically bullied, do not encourage fighting back. I know some fathers, at least in respect of their sons, tend to think that 'to give as good as you get and more' will sort everything out, even though they may have no knowledge about the strength or the number of bullies involved. What needs to be borne in mind before giving advice is that if your son or daughter could fight off the 'bully(s)', they would have done so at the outset when they were first targeted. The fact that they have picked up the courage to tell you means that they are unable to beat them off physically. Expecting them to fight back when they feel they have no chance

only compounds any feelings of inadequacy they may already have about their physical strength. It may also prompt them to no longer confide in you for fear of being perceived as weak. Instead suggest the following strategies:

- If the physical attack is preceded by provocative taunts, respond with assertiveness, which can include giving a clear intention of reporting it if an attack should follow (see Information Box below).
- If they sense the possibility of an imminent physical attack, walk over to a friend, a group or a teacher, or loudly proclaim or shout, 'Don't you dare touch me or I'll report you'.
- If the physical attacks happen out of the blue without any forewarning, let the bully(s) know that it will be reported. This needs to be followed up by you as a parent to see if appropriate action was taken. Make note of the date of the report and the date and nature of the school's response.

Information Box: Teaching Your Child to Stand up to Bullying
- Act confident.
- Don't hit out.
- Remember it's not about you.
- Fix them with your eye.
- Stand tall.
- Talk your way out of it.
- Use humour.
- Use 'I' messages: 'I want you to stop ...' instead of, 'You are a ...'.
- Walk away at an average pace and with your head held up.
- Report behaviour to a friend, a teacher and a parent.

Extortion Bullying

If bullying takes the form of extortion, it is important that your child tries to cut down on the opportunities that the bully has to corner him or her. If there are threatening cyber-messages, these should be kept as evidence of the extortion when reporting the problem. Also, encourage your child not to take valuable possessions to school, as they can become a source of great envy. They should also be encouraged to have all possessions that they take to school visibly marked with a permanent pen, as this makes them less attractive for extortion.

Should the extortion bullying involve handing over valuable items, lunches or money, and if your child is threatened with injury if they don't 'cough up', advise your child to meet the request. No possession is more valuable than safety, but make sure that they are empowered to report it. Schools should welcome such reports because it will allow them to discipline the offenders.

If negative or anti-social behaviour is extorted, such as having to commit an anti-social act in order to be allowed to be part of the peer group, advise an assertive response. Teach them the value of being true to themselves and not to compromise their values for the sake of being popular. They need to appreciate that being sucked into doing something that is against their better judgement will invariably lead to hurting someone. Explain that any person that demands unacceptable behaviour as proof of loyalty may not be worth having as a friend. Suggest they should seek more like-minded peers to have as friends. Once one member has had the courage to stand up to the negative peer pressure from an individual or group, it is not unusual for others to break away and together form a new group that holds more positive values.

Name-Calling

Name-calling is the most common form of direct bullying and can be extremely nasty and humiliating. It threatens a child or teenager's identity and sense of self, as it can throw disparaging remarks about almost anything, like your child's looks, sexuality, ability, personality, religion, family members, culture, ethnic background and nationality.[1] It is vital to stress to your child that hearing something said about them does not mean that it is true or that they have to believe it. Remind your child that it says more about the 'bully's' prejudices and troubled mind than it does about theirs. You can also have your child visualise having dirt thrown at him/her; the intention of the aggressor is always to have the dirt stick, but it can be washed off. And so it is with verbal bullying. The 'bully' wants a hurt response and not one where he/she is left looking foolish. From the Information Box below you will see that your child should, if at all possible, show no sign of upset and respond with assertiveness and/or humour. Possible humorous responses to all forms of name-calling can be practised and role played at home, as can developing assertiveness. Also empowering is to have your child write down all that young people say about each other that is hurtful. This helps to greatly depersonalise and take the sting out of verbal bullying.

Most important, however, is for your child to know that should they feel unable to stop the name-calling by their own efforts, they should feel no shame in reporting it. Let them know that they will only be doing the individual bully(s) a favour by doing so, as it will afford the perpetrator an opportunity to have their problems addressed by the school, and hopefully in a restorative way that will teach them how to manage their emotions in a more responsible manner.

Information Box: How to Deal with Verbal Bullying

- Try not to show how upset or hurt you feel as it encourages the 'bully', making them feel like they have the power.
- Practise non-verbal behaviour, which conveys an assertive response or one that shows whatever was said just bounced off you and fell like a bad throw at a dartboard. Try, for example, to shrug your shoulders and throw your eyes up as if to say, 'You know, you are so sad' or, 'Would you get a life!'
- The key to an effective response is to deflect the negative attention back to the 'bully', leaving the perpetrator lost for words: 'Look who's talking'; 'What's your problem?'; 'It takes one to know another'. A very effective response to sexual innuendos is, 'Join the club' or, 'Go check out your problems with a counsellor'.

Exclusion

Being excluded is one of the most painful experiences there can be because, as I pointed out in Part One, a child is desperate to belong to a group. It gives them an identity, provides predictability and a sense of security and safety. To be rejected leaves children and young people feeling extremely rejected, insecure and vulnerable. Girls are particularly vulnerable to exclusion as they use relational bullying as a weapon more often than boys. However, it needs to be borne in mind that relational bullying can also easily escalate to physical bullying unless stopped.

Once again, as with the other forms of bullying, it is important to stress to your child or teenager the causes of bullying in order to prevent any self-blame that they might be harbouring. Remember that jealousy, insecurity and unhappiness is a cause of a lot of bullying. When talking about the repeated attempts by a 'bully' to isolate your child, try to find out who the ringleader might be (i.e. the queen bee) and then the others in the group (i.e. the wannabees) who support the ringleader.

Talk about the dynamics of peer pressure (see p. 182). Discuss whether it is worth trying to befriend the group if there is such a lack of respect and true friendship, and whether there are opportunities for new friendships outside of the group. If the isolation should persist, no shame should be felt in reporting it to the school. The group involved should then be taken aside and with good restorative practice be expected to make amends.

Cyber-Bullying

Cyber-bullying takes many forms and as technology advances we can expect many more forms to emerge. Sadly, parents need to look no further than to the high-profile cases I mentioned earlier of teenagers Phoebe Prince in Massachusetts and Leanne Wolfe in Ireland to appreciate the depths of despair that can result from cyber-bullying, especially when it is used alongside traditional forms of bullying. This left both girls unable to escape their tormentor's repeated and venomous attacks. I am sure a lot of people can identify with that sinking feeling when a hateful message pops up whenever you go to use your mobile phone, e-mail or log on to chat to some friends on a favourite social networking site. To have it happening time and time again eats relentlessly away at you.

Prevention is Better than Cure

We all know that prevention is better than cure, but surprisingly we tend to be slow in putting it into practice and as a result end up dealing with problems that could have been avoided. It is important to recognise that children can spend seven hours or more a day in electronic life. From the moment they wake up and until going through the school gates they are sending and receiving texts, listening to their iPods and, once out of school and at home, they are back online again. If, as parents, you have concerns about internet safety and cyber-bullying, the best you can do to safeguard your child or teenager from engaging in or being a victim of cyber-abuse is as follows:

- Inform yourself about internet use and safety. Read the booklets 'Get With It', published by the Internet Safety Office, Ireland. These booklets are also accessible online (www.internetsafety.ie). You can also become acquainted with the cyber language used by young people (for example, TDTM: talk dirty to me) by visiting http://en.wikipedia.org/wiki/Internet_slang. If you are not very computer literate, ask your child or teen to teach you. They will feel proud to be asked and it is a great way to engage them in a conversation about internet safety and online behaviour.

- Inform yourself about blocking devices. There is an increasing amount of blocking devices coming on the market that can stop unfriendly text messages and calls from getting through to your child's phone (see, for example, vMad's Bully Stop).

- Emphasise responsible use of the internet. Do not take for granted that your child or teenager knows how to stay safe on the internet or how to contact their service provider. Marion Finnegan, a teacher and student of Trinity College's Master of Education (Aggression Studies), found that almost one-third of transition year students were not sure when or how to contact their service provider. Make sure that they also understand how file sharing and taking text, images, artwork or music from the web may infringe on copyright laws.

- Talk about their online friends and activities in the same way that you would about traditional friendships and activities. Remember the many positive uses of the internet. Cyberspace can help children who have difficulties in establishing good face-to-face relationships in the real world to develop their social interaction skills and friendships that might otherwise prove difficult (for example, children with autism, Asperger Syndrome, ADHD or social phobia).

- Make sure they are aware of the dangers of giving out personal information. They should ask themselves whether they would post the same information in a shop window or a message board in a supermarket.

- Emphasise the concept 'never do onto others what you would not like done to yourself'. This empathic statement and value should be like a broken record within every home. In respect of cyber-bullying, it is especially important not to initiate, engage with peers or

203

forward on any nasty comments or video clips. Talk to your child about ethical behaviour. Explain the hurt and despair that cyber-bullying can cause the victim.

- Stress that cyber-bullying is wrong and is the action of cowards. Those who engage in cyber-bullying, such as persistently spreading gossip and posting demeaning messages, need to know that their behaviour says more about them than it does about the victim; it reflects a lack of social or emotional stability, poor moral reasoning and/or an inability to withstand peer pressure.

- Stress that cyber-bullying can lead to a criminal offence. Any person that sends a text message or internet communication that is grossly offensive or harasses another person risks being guilty of an offence.

- Do not over-police. To limit and excessively monitor the use of the internet can cause unnecessary resentment and drive the behaviour underground. Remember your child can access it through friends' houses and internet cafes. Build trust and an open climate instead. If you find out that they have breached your trust, withdraw the privilege of the internet for a stated time period.

- Stress that if in doubt, they should seek help. Let them know that you will always be there for them should they feel worried or threatened by messages or material that they have come across on the internet. Remember boys are more likely than girls to push the boundaries looking for activities and sites that are explicit and sensational.

- Be alert to changes in mood and behaviour. Tell-tale signs of being cyber-bullied are showing upset or anger while on a mobile phone or online, or after receiving a call, text or logging off.

Steps to Take if Your Child is Being Cyber-Bullied

If you have concerns that your child or teenager may be a victim of cyber-bullying, proceed as you would with traditional bullying, for example, by alerting the school to your concerns.

Should you discover that your child is being cyber-bullied, remain calm, gain as much information as you can about the nature of the cyber-bullying, who is involved and whether traditional bullying is also involved. Talk through all the possible self-help strategies for being bullied by phone or over the internet. There is plenty of online advice on how to react to cyber-bullying. All the websites[2] emphasise that cyber-bullying can be stopped and that it can usually be traced. Thus, it is important for children not to ignore it but to tell someone or call an advice line for guidance. No matter which medium is used to cyber-bully (text/video messaging, phone calls, e-mails, web bullying, chat rooms and instant messaging) it is important that your child understands the following key points:

- Do not be ashamed. The shame lies with the tormentors.
- Do not reply. An emotional reaction is just what the tormentor(s) are hoping for and gives them cause for further harassment.
- Save offensive or threatening messages or video clips as evidence. Learn to do a screen grab by saving the entire screen that holds the offensive messages or pictures. Try not to repeat reading them or dwell on them. Brainstorm solutions instead.
- Don't hang up immediately on abusive or silent phone calls. See if you recognise the caller's number. Walk away from the phone. The caller will get fed up and, unable to get an emotional reaction, will stop the harassment.
- Report cyber-bullying to parents or teachers. They can help to discern whether there is merit in reporting the cyber-bullying to the police.

Rebuilding Your Child or Teenager's Self-Image

There is nothing more guaranteed to rob your child or teenager of their confidence and lower their self-esteem than being picked on, whether directly or indirectly, day in and day out by one or more of their peers. Oversensitivity, agitation, irritability and a misinterpretation of comments and questions from you or any other member of the family is a sign of a damaged self-esteem. Indeed, they may take questions of concern and interest in their welfare as a personal attack on their ability to cope. However, as a parent there is much you can do to rebuild your child's confidence and help him/her regain a sense of well-being.

More than ever before you will need to give your child extra time, attention, unconditional love, approval and praise. Make sure that the other members of the family are also positive in their behaviour towards him/her (see preceding chapter on tips for enhancing self-esteem). If you should find that your efforts are not having the desired effect, consider seeking professional psychological support, such as counselling or cognitive behavioural therapy.

Dealing With Thoughts of Suicide

Thoughts of suicide, as I explained in Part One, are not uncommon among bullied children and teenagers. It has been reported that children as young as six years of age have attempted suicide.[3] Should you notice signs of deep despair, expressions of revenge, alcohol or drug abuse, self-harming or talk of suicide, do not hesitate to alert the school and seek professional help (see Information Box below for warning signs of suicide).

Parents should never fear that by asking their child or teenager if they have thoughts of suicide that they are putting thoughts into their head. Children are generally relieved that the subject has been brought up and that there is someone who cares and is willing to talk about it. If your child should admit to feelings of suicide, best practice would be to do the following:

- Do not dismiss your child's feelings. Don't say, 'You mustn't think that way.' Instead, encourage them to talk about their feelings and thoughts without passing judgement.
- Be honest. If your child's behaviour scares or worries you say so. Make sure your child knows how much you care and how devastating it would be for you and the family if something happened to them. Let them know that you will be there for them and do whatever it takes to make them happy again.
- Do not leave your child alone until you are confident that they are getting back to their former selves.

Information Box: Warning Signs of Suicide
- A significant change in behaviour (depressed demeanour, loss of energy, rarely smiling, missing classes or school, dropping out of school, no interest in appearance or personal hygiene.
- A significant change in appetite, sudden weight gain or loss.
- Change in sleep patterns, inability to sleep, waking up early or oversleeping.

206

- Agitation, difficulty concentrating and sitting still, very restless.
- A loss of interest in friends.
- Persistent feelings of hopelessness, worthlessness, full of self-hate.
- Excessive risk-taking.
- Getting affairs in order, giving away possessions.
- Mood lift (can occur when the decision has been made to commit suicide as there is relief that a solution has been found to stop the agony).

Dealing With Anxiety and Post-Traumatic Stress Disorder (PTSD)

Strong anxiety and, indeed, symptoms of post-traumatic stress can result from severe bullying incidents that have left the victim desperately shaken, if not fearful for their lives. Children and adolescents who suffer from post-traumatic stress disorder find their social and emotional lives turned upside down. They frequently relive their traumatic experiences through flashbacks and nightmares. Thoughts, feelings, activities, situations or people who are associated with the trauma may also be deliberately forgotten or avoided. Often the mere thought of bumping into someone associated with the traumatic events or seeing them in the distance may be enough to arouse severe anxiety or a panic attack. PTSD can significantly impair the child's ability to function socially, especially outside of the home.

Should you feel that anxiety, depression and symptoms of PTSD are issues for your child, seek professional help. Cognitive behavioural therapy (CBT) is a great way to help young people overcome their anxiety. CBT is a practical approach that concentrates on current events and difficulties. It is based on the premise that it is our thoughts that determine our feelings and, in turn, it is our feelings that determine our behaviour. The challenge is to change the way we think, as that will change our feelings and, thus, our behaviour will change. The therapist will help your child find:

- the anxious thoughts and feelings that he/she has;
- the link between what your child thinks, how he/she feels and what he/she does;
- more helpful ways of thinking that make your child feel less anxious;
- how to face and overcome their problems.[4]

Changing Schools

If the bullying continues in spite of your intervention, that of the school or that of some external professional support, you may need to consider changing schools. Your first priority has to be that of protecting your child. However, before making such a decision you will need to take the child's wishes into account so that the advantages outweigh any disadvantages. Remember, teenagers find it more difficult to change schools and leave their peer group behind than younger children. Make sure that the schools you may be considering have a comprehensive anti-bullying policy and a culture that does not tolerate bullying. Make sure also that you make known the reasons for the change in schools so that they can take all the necessary precautions to prevent any reoccurrence of bullying. Hopefully they may have some peer support scheme such as 'mentoring' or 'befriending', which should make it easier for your child to settle in and make new friends (see Chapter 12).

Key Messages

- To be bullied, whether in a traditional way, by cyber methods or both, is very upsetting and can cause many disturbing behavioural and performance-related changes.
- Children do not admit readily to being bullied, so if concerned, probe in a gentle and non-judgemental manner to draw them out. Displaying undue emotion and overreacting will not help them to open up.
- If you are worried but your child denies being bullied, talk to the parents of your child's friends or the school itself to see whether they can throw any light on your concerns.
- If you are still worried but faced with little evidence of bullying, depending on the age of your child, talk through some of the well-known self-help skills on prevention and intervention of traditional and cyber-bullying or encourage them to read a self-help book for themselves.
- If cyber-bullied, keep copies and a record of any cyber-bullying activity. Learn to do a screen grab, save text messages, e-mails and so on.
- Do not dwell on what was said or done. Instead, brainstorm solutions.

- Before approaching your child's school, become informed of their anti-bullying policy and procedures for reporting.
- When talking to the relevant staff or principal, resist taking a critical and judgemental approach.
- Give the school time to investigate and report back to you.
- Keep a record of all discussions with the school, including dates and times.
- Work with the school to seek solutions to stop the bullying.
- Should the symptoms of bullying still persist, such as anxiety, anger, post-traumatic stress, depression and thoughts of suicide, seek professional psychological help.
- Keep your school informed of any therapeutic treatment your child may be receiving.
- Should the bullying still persist in spite of all efforts or lack of effort on the part of the school, consider changing schools.

Notes

1. See DVDs, *Silent Witnesses* or *Bully for You*.
2. www.respectme.org, www.kidscape.org and www.wiresafety.org.
3. *Irish Times*, 29 August 2007.
4. For more details about CBT and how to beat anxiety problems in children and adolescents, see Paul Stallard's book, *Anxiety: Cognitive Behaviour Therapy with Children and Young People*, London: Routledge, 2009.

STEPS TO TAKE IF YOU SUSPECT YOUR CHILD IS BULLYING OTHERS

It is undoubtedly an understatement to say that most parents or guardians would be dismayed and upset to hear that their child or teenager was engaging in bullying behaviour. To be labelled a 'bully' conjures up an image that is negative and distasteful. Sadly, it also carries a poor prognosis, placing happy long-term relationships and good job prospects at risk. Thus, parents who have their children's future at heart would be doing them a huge favour if they nipped all bullying behaviour in the bud. As parents, this means not only challenging bullying behaviour that they see, but also responding positively to complaints of alleged bullying from teachers or other parents. Hearing that one's child has been a ringleader or assisted in bullying a fellow student should not be met with shame, because the reasons for bullying can be many. We tend to forget that childhood and adolescence is about learning, and that includes learning how to behave in a respectful manner. Therefore, shame is only appropriate and should be reserved for situations where no action is taken to deal with complaints of bullying.

As bullying is often transient and an expression of some form of stress, feelings of worthlessness, frustration, insecurity, lack of love, attention and recognition, it can so easily be put right if sufficient attention is given to the causative factors. The earlier this is done the better in order to prevent the negative behaviours from becoming habitual and chronic. Below you will find possible warning signs that your child may bully others.

> **Information Box: Warning Signs that Your Child May Bully Others**
> - Reacts to frustration in an aggressive manner.
> - Quick to tease, slag and use 'put downs'.
> - Cruel to pets.

- Disruptive, defiant and rude to adults.
- Enjoys feeling powerful and in control.
- Seems to get pleasure from hurting others.
- Blames others for wrongdoing.
- Attention-seeking and satisfied whether it is negative or positive.
- Acts cool and hangs around with a gang.
- Drawn towards risk-taking and anti-social activities.

Steps to Dealing with Bullying

1. Examine Your Style of Discipline

Children very often model their behaviour on that of their parents. Therefore, it would be worthwhile to examine your style of discipline. Might it be too harsh and inconsistent? Remember that physical punishment tends to be only therapeutic for the person releasing their feelings of frustration and anger. It does little for the offending child, other than build up a reservoir of resentment and indignity while at the same time showing them that 'might makes right'. A more effective method to promote positive behaviour is for parents to respond to inappropriate behaviour in a firm, fair and respectful manner. The Information Box below gives a quick guide to assertive discipline for parents.[1] Signing up to a parenting courses can also be very effective in helping to establish a positive and assertive discipline style.

Information Box : Assertive Discipline for Parents

- Decide rules and discipline in advance.
- Keep the rules you insist on with your child or teen to the minimum.
- Agree with your child or teen on what is fair when there is a breach of rules.
- If rules are broken, follow through with the consequences.
- Use 'I' messages, for example, 'I want you to stop screaming at Jack now. Try to calm down. If you still cannot sort out your differences, tell me what the row is about and I'll try to help'; 'I want you to do your homework now, so you will be finished before going out to play/meet your friends'.
- Reward with praise or some token when your request is met. Tokens, be they stars, stickers or ticks on a board, can be traded in for a privilege, such as an outing, a visit to a favourite shop, the cinema or extra pocket money.
- If your child or teen does not comply after repeating your request calmly, give him/her a warning. They should know that you will allow only two warnings. This is similar to the well-known yellow card/red card method used in sports.
- If the warnings have no effect, impose a negative consequence, for example, less pocket money for the week or cut back on TV viewing or internet use.
- Be a good role model. Actions speak louder than words.

2. Identify Any Unmet Emotional Needs that Your Child May Have

Children who feel overlooked, taken for granted or under pressure to succeed can so easily take their frustrations and resentment out on others. Spend quality time with them. Make them feel special. Love them for who they are and not for what you feel they can or should achieve. Catch them when they are good and reward them for desired behaviour whenever possible. Remember, the carrot works better than the stick. Take every opportunity to enhance their self-esteem (see Chapter 8 for guidance).

3. Look to Your Child's Social Skills

Might there be any deficiencies in these, such as the ability to listen, follow rules of play, apologise, help others, share, be a good sport, understand the feelings of others, deal with group pressure or manage conflict and anger. Children who lack these social skills may be unaware of the effect of their behaviour on others. As a result, they may say the wrong thing at the wrong time or have difficulty forming strong friendships. Children with autism and Asperger Syndrome tend to lack certain social skills and would certainly benefit from social skills training. Any deficiencies in social skills can be corrected through teaching and role play (see p. 216 for details on how to provide social skills training and p. 160 on aggression replacement training).

4. Give Your Child Something to Excel In

Affording your child an opportunity to excel in something that they are interested in, like sport, martial arts, music, drama or volunteering, can often change their outlook and behaviour. Excelling in something will help them to gain recognition and approval. Doing well in something makes a child feel good and this can help to lose any sense of inferiority, which may trigger jealousy and prompt them to impose their frustrations on their fellow students. Remember, 'enter through the door of their interest and you will exit through the door of your objective'.[2] Success breeds success and the contentment that follows reduces the need to put others down in order to feel good.

5. Look to Your Child's Ability to Manage Anger

Every act of aggression has multiple causes, stemming from societal to individual ones. While anger is a natural human emotion, the expectation is that children will learn to respond to their impulsive feelings in a manner that is not offensive and hurtful to others with words, physical force or weapons. If they cannot successfully manage their anger, it is because they may not be, a) fully aware of what triggers the anger, b) recognise the mental and physical changes that are felt and c) know the techniques to use to defuse the anger. Any or all of these deficiencies can be taught by you as a parent or by outside agencies specialising in anger management (see section on anger management later in this chapter).

6. Look to Your Child's Sense of Values and Moral Reasoning

Much aggression and bullying in childhood reflects the absence of good moral reasoning. It is generally accepted that moral reasoning is dependent on age and cognitive ability. Young children below four or five years of age have little awareness of rules. However, from age four or five to around nine or ten, moral realism becomes evident. This means that the rules that are set are the ones to be obeyed irrespective of the circumstances. After the age of nine or ten, children begin to evaluate rules and judge actions according to the circumstances and intentions of the perpetrator. Children who bully tend to have poor moral reasoning. For example, they often rationalise and justify their aggressive behaviour by blaming the victim for what has happened to avoid taking responsibility. If they are part of a group or gang they will blame it on the others. They may also show little guilt and little or no empathy for their victims. As parents, it is vital that all rationalisations and justifications for inappropriate aggression and bullying are tackled. Should you be witness to or hear of hurtful behaviour that your child has committed, do not let it go unchallenged. Encourage them to see the wrong in their behaviour and to take responsibility for their actions and find some way to make amends. It is important also to take some time to have them consider and talk to you about how they might feel if they were bullied. Asking your child to put themselves in another's shoes will help to strengthen their ability to empathise. A child who can do this well is unlikely to victimise their fellow students. There is no better way to instil good moral values and empathy in children than to lead by example. All too often as adults we are inclined to engage in double standards, leaving children to witness what may often be disrespectful and hurtful behaviour (for further guidance on moral reasoning see p. 161).

7. Teach Respect for Diversity

Children who bully very often believe it is fair game to point the finger at and pick on peers whose behaviour does not match their own traditional standards and beliefs, be they social, economic, sexual, cultural or racial. Beliefs and prejudices generally have their roots in society, yet find support in the home and through print or screen media. The sooner we teach our children that there is richness in diversity, that it is the personal attributes of the people they meet that matters and not which class or creed they belong to, the sooner we will prevent our children from feeling threatened by what is 'different'.

In my co-authored book with Stephen James Minton, *Dealing with Bullying in School: A Training Manual for Teachers, Parents and Other Professionals*, we set out an exercise that parents can use to great effect if you find that your child tends to harass fellow students due to a lack of respect for individual differences and beliefs.

The exercise is as follows. Take a current news item from TV, radio, a newspaper or magazine dealing with people from a different culture or religion. Choose one 'ordinary person', preferably of a similar age to your child, to focus on. Ask the following questions:

- What do you think you have in common with this person?
- Who do you think this person lives with and in what sort of house?
- What sort of school do you think he/she goes to?
- How do you think they spend their time after school, at weekends, during holidays?
- What wishes, dreams or ambitions do you think he/she has?
- What would you like to ask him/her given the chance? And what do you think he/she would like to ask you?
- Do you think you could get to like this person?

The aim of an exercise such as this is to help children learn to challenge stereotypes by having them focus on the similarities rather than the differences. In time they will appreciate that, in spite of superficial differences, they have more in common with people than they may have believed.

8. Use Screen Violence Positively

There is strong scientific evidence that those who observe violence are more likely to behave more violently, both in the short term and long term. Exposure, for example, to violent video games leads to an increase in aggressive thoughts, feelings and behaviour. Moreover, there is an increase in physiological arousal and a decrease in pro-social behaviour. Most worthy of attention is that exposure to media violence in childhood stimulates aggressive behaviour in later years. It is, therefore, tempting to say that you should try to limit the amount of screen violence that your child watches or actively engages in (for example, playing video games). However, should this prove difficult for practical reasons (you are at work, your child has a TV in their bedroom) or if it causes friction and struggle, then make sure that you let your views be known about violence.

Hopefully your views will reflect disapproval of violence. Children who grow up in homes and neighbourhoods where violence is not tolerated will not be as accepting of violence as those who witness violence in their homes and neighbourhoods. To ensure that your child appreciates the cost of violence to individuals, families and society, take an interest in the films or games that occupy your child's attention and take time to discuss them. Like the previous exercise on developing respect for individual differences and diversity, you can encourage your child to focus on the individual characters in the film, for example, the hero, the villain or the victim. You can have lots of fun with them exchanging views on the rights and wrongs of the screen character's behaviour and what it must feel like to come out on top as opposed to being defeated. Equally, have them consider how it would all pan out in real life. For example, on the screen we see people survive the most hideous beatings and shootings and rarely are the aggressors apprehended and punished. As young children especially tend to take things literally, it is important that they learn from their parents to appreciate the serious consequences of aggression and that there are alternatives to violence in solving problems.

In helping your child to become more media literate and especially to become more critical of violence and to distinguish reality from fantasy, you will give them a keener sense of the futility of violence. Also, it will help them to better appreciate the values that are needed for the good of society.

Social Skills Training

Common to all social skills training programmes are the following steps.

1. Provide Instruction

In choosing, for example, the social skill of 'understanding the feelings of others', which is generally referred to as empathy, you would approach it by describing the desired behaviour in precise terms. This means talking through each step of the skill and allowing your child to perform it as follows:

- Watch the other person and take note of their tone of voice, posture and facial expression.
- Listen to what the other person is saying and try to understand it.
- Figure out what the person might be feeling. Is the person, for example, anxious, sad, annoyed or excited?
- Show that you understand what the person is feeling. You may say something appropriate, touch the person or signal your understanding by some appropriate non-verbal gesture.

2. Model the Behaviour

Demonstrate for your child or teenager the desired behaviour so that they can see exactly the steps that are involved. A good way is also to take advantage of TV viewing with your child or teenager so you can point to characters who demonstrate the desired social skill.

3. Practise the Skills

By practising what has been taught and with good feedback, children will soon get the hang of it and, with time, they will be encouraged and reinforced in their efforts because of the positive and friendly responses they will experience when they exercise good social skills. An effective way to practise this is for you and other members of the family to role play the desired skills. For example, you can have one member of the family take on the empathic role while the other takes on the role of someone lacking in empathy and vice versa. The best results are achieved when everyone is clear about the specific behaviours that are to be performed.[3]

Anger Management

The best way to teach your child to manage anger is to encourage him or her to keep a diary or log of all angry outbursts at home and at school on a daily basis. If your child finds this difficult, you can at least jot down the angry incidents that occur at home. Your child's 'hassle log' or your own notes should provide a good basis for helping your child understand the A-B-C of anger.

The 'A' of anger relates to the triggers: when, where, what or who causes the anger? Anger is always an emotional reaction to something. However, it does not have to be something real. It can be triggered by thoughts and perceptions. For example, if a fellow student were to bump into your child, they could either accept it as an accident or think no more about it, or they could perceive it as an intentional act and thus feel justified in reacting with anger. It is perhaps helpful to think of your child's anger as being one of three things, which are as follows:[4]

- A response to frustration when your child's needs are not being met. Consider your child's reaction to being thwarted when they are not readily understood or they do not get what they want (an expensive toy in a toyshop), or your adolescent son or daughter if you insist that they cannot go to a party except at weekends, and even then they must be home by a certain hour. A good word for describing the 'causes' of this type of anger is, therefore, 'thwarted'.
- A response to getting what we want. This form of anger is known as 'instrumental anger' and is used by children in a calculating or sneaky way to get what they want. A young child may, for example, throw a temper tantrum in order to get their way, or adolescents may storm out of a room angrily, threatening to run away from home

or quit school. It is this form of deliberate anger that children who bully frequently use to intimidate and frighten their victims into submission.

- A release of pent-up emotions. This type of anger is known as 'cathartic anger' and is commonly used as a safety valve, providing children with a means to release their pent-up emotions. When they are at the end of their tether or they feel powerless to change things, or the situation seems hopeless for them and they are overwhelmed by events, they essentially explode and feel better for it.

The 'B' of anger relates to the cues: how the body reacts when feeling angry, for example, what mental, physical and behavioural changes are felt when anger is building up? To help your child stop the build-up of anger, he/she needs to tune in to the early warning signs, which most often tend to be the tensing of muscles, clenched fists and teeth or a pounding heart.

The 'C' of anger relates to understanding the consequences of anger for both the aggressor and those targeted. In keeping a hassle log, the nature of the angry outburst and the problems that so often result from a show of bad anger (punishments and disciplinary action) will become much clearer. Once children recognise that bad anger generally creates more problems than it solves, they will be more open to learning ways to better control and manage their anger.

Introduce 'Anger Reducers' or 'Anger Spoilers'

There are three techniques that are very effective in reducing anger. They are known as 'anger reducers' or 'anger spoilers'. They can be easily modelled by you and taught to your child, who should be encouraged and reminded to use them whenever he/she becomes aware of the triggers and the warning signs of anger.

1. Deep Breathing

This is at the heart of all relaxation therapies, from Transcendental Meditation to Zen and Yoga. Simply ask your child to practise taking a few deep breaths. When breathing in suggest they can count to seven and when breathing out they can count to eleven. This is known as seven/eleven breathing.

2. Backward Counting

Advise your child when he/she is faced with a provocative person or situation, which they find has the potential for an out-of-control or angry response, to turn away and count backwards slowly from twenty to one. This will reduce the tension and increase personal control.

3. Pleasant Imagery

Have your child seek an image that conjures up pure joy and relaxation. Practise visualising this scene and tune into it when there is a build-up of emotions.

Introduce Reminders

Reminders are self-instructional statements used to help increase success in pressure or volatile situations of all kinds. The authors of *Aggression Replacement Training* place a lot of emphasis on reminders to help control thoughts, feelings and behaviour. Examples of self-instructional statements are, 'cool it', 'chill it', 'relax', 'calm it' and 'take it easy'. Reminders can also take the form of a positive interpretation of what might otherwise be taken to be an intentionally provocative act ('he didn't knock into me on purpose, he tripped or he wasn't watching where he was going'). Most effective are the reminders that your child or teenager creates for themselves.

To get your child used to using reminders, model them as you would the anger reducers in your everyday living. For example, when you recognise the cues of anger, take a few deep breaths, count backwards or conjure up a pleasant scene and give yourself a reminder such as 'cool it, getting angry won't help'. Practise makes perfect and you can have fun with your children exploring which anger-reducing technique and which reminder works best for them at home and in school.

Finally, to strengthen your efforts to introduce your child to any of the above techniques to deal better with anger, do not overlook the value of self-help books and relevant internet material. To help six- to twelve-year-olds, for example, to understand and manage their frustrations and anger, you will find Fiona McAuslan and Peter Nicholson's *Resolving Anger* book most useful (see Recommended Reading).

A Special Note: The Relaxation Response

While it is not essential for defusing anger, in my opinion it is the ultimate in preventing and managing threatening and highly charged or stressful situations. Once mastered it is a fantastic bonus and self-help skill for life. It can bring inner peace and calm in the same way that an appropriate and well-chosen prayer can. Mastering the Relaxation Response enables one to take a much more relaxed attitude to people and situations that would ordinarily be threatening or upsetting. Most often it is the perspective and attribution to events that change. What earlier may have been perceived as hostile (a fellow student bumping into your child) and would, therefore, have triggered an angry response, with the Relaxation Response it is more likely that the same experience will be met with a shrug of the shoulders and a self-statement to the effect of, 'What has gotten into him today?'

Anyone can learn the Relaxation Response. It requires no special educational requirement or aptitude. You may find that your child already knows it, as I know of some teachers who start their classes with having the students use a relaxation technique. Below you will find what I believe to be the most straightforward technique, which can be easily self-taught. I recommend it to anyone who is unable for financial and other reasons to sign up to a relaxation course (for example, autogenic training, transcendental meditation or yoga). Dr Herbert Benson, Associate Professor of Medicine at Harvard Medical School and Director of the Hypertension Section of Boston's Beth Israel Hospital, developed and used the technique with great success on his patients. If you give it a go and practise it daily and encourage your family to learn it, I would be very surprised to hear that it did not help both you and your family to deal with your daily stresses in a more calm and relaxed manner.

The steps to eliciting the Relaxation Response are as follows:[5]

- Sit quietly in a comfortable position.
- Close your eyes.
- Deeply relax all your muscles, beginning at your feet and progressing up to your face. Keep them relaxed.
- Breathe through your nose. Become aware of your breathing. As you breathe out, say the word, 'ONE' clearly to yourself. For example,

breathe in ... out ... 'ONE' ... in ... out ... 'ONE', and so on. Breathe easily and naturally.
- Continue for ten to twenty minutes. You may open your eyes to check the time, but do not use an alarm. When you finish, sit quietly for several minutes, at first with your eyes closed and later with your eyes open. Do not stand up for a few minutes.

It is important to recognise that there is no need to worry about whether you are successful in achieving a deep level of relaxation. Simply maintain a passive attitude and permit relaxation to occur at its own pace. When distracting thoughts occur, try to ignore them by not dwelling on them and return to repeating 'ONE'. With practice, the response should come with little effort. The technique should be practised once or twice daily, but Dr Benson recommends not practising it within two hours after any meal, since the digestive processes seem to interfere with the elicitation of the Relaxation Response.

It should be noted that the word 'ONE' is simply a device to distract you from your thoughts, which means that you can choose a word of your own instead, which then will act as your unique mantra. Once the body and mind has learned (been conditioned) to associate the word 'ONE', or another chosen word, with the Relaxation Response, the word alone can be called upon to act as a stimulus to relax. It is a most economic and healthy substitute to drug-induced relaxation and can be used to combat all forms of stress, from fear of performing on stage, being wronged or insulted, to road rage.

Key Messages
- Aggression, bullying and violence in childhood and adolescent years increase the risks of later social, emotional and behavioural difficulties, educational underachievement and job opportunities.
- Look to the cause of the bullying and you will find the cure.
- As parents, model positive parenting.
- Build respect and tolerance for individual differences and diversity.
- Play to your child's strengths and build a sturdy self-esteem by providing ample opportunities for success and recognition.

- Make sure your family know you love them for who they are (unconditional love) and not for what they can achieve (conditional love).
- Build empathy, enhance social skills, teach anger management and strengthen moral reasoning.
- To correct specific deficiencies that cause bullying behaviours, do not hesitate to seek independent help and support from appropriate agencies.

Notes

1. To read more about positive parenting, please refer to *Positive Parenting* by John Sharry, Dublin: Veritas, 2008.

2. This was a view held by the late Prof. Peter Dempsey of the Department of Applied Psychology, University College Cork. He was of the firm opinion that the key concept, the central, all-important idea in the learning process is interest. As a young colleague at the time, I heard him proclaim, 'We must make every intelligent effort to arouse and maintain interest in the task, scatter many wares before the student and watch where the eye glistens.' This has guided my philosophy of teaching ever since.

3. For further details on how to teach social skills, refer to *Aggression Replacement Training* (ART) by Goldstein, Glick and Gibbs (see Recommended Reading). Their book includes a checklist for parents that will help to identify the social skills that may need to be enhanced in order to minimise conflict and inappropriate aggression. It also provides instruction on how to teach each of the social skills.

4. See Faupel, Herrick and Sharp, *Anger Management: A Practical Guide* (see Recommended Reading).

5. Benson, H. and Klipper, M., *The Relaxation Response*, Glasgow: Collins Fount Paperbacks, 1984.

FINAL WORD

The purpose of this book was to deepen your understanding of victimisation and bullying in the hope that you, as readers, would seize every opportunity to counter and prevent it.

Whereas the book is predominantly directed at teachers and parents, I also strongly believe that bullying is everyone's problem. The more people in society that can be persuaded to dispel the myths surrounding bullying, the sooner we can make life better for all children. I feel that I cannot impress upon readers enough the destructive nature of bullying. By ignoring the problem we are sentencing both victims and bullies to lives that are blighted by feelings of inferiority, unhappiness and underachievement. Bystanders to bullying incidents are also often left to suffer from bouts of anxiety and guilt due to their lack of intervention.

As adults, it is vital that we see bullying as an activity and not a stereotypical role. In that way, by taking corrective action to prevent or reduce bullying we can help children change their behaviour in a way that affords them the opportunity and the skills to develop healthy relationships. When children are happy and feel respected, valued and safe, they will be more inclined to release their energy in a positive, constructive and creative manner, which can only benefit society. Most importantly, they will be better able to concentrate and, thus, benefit from the many learning activities that schools have to offer. Therefore, by challenging bullying whenever it comes to our attention and offering the necessary constructive and rehabilitative solutions, we are giving our school-going population the best possible chance of realising their personal and vocational ambitions.

If you, as a reader, are not a parent or teacher, you can still make a significant difference in preventing and reducing bullying among young people by lending your voice to saying 'No' to bullying. Remember, there should be nothing cool, worthy or honourable about crushing a fellow human being. We must all appreciate that as long as bullying is condoned by society, every individual, whether child or adult, is at risk of suffering some form of direct or indirect bullying. No one is immune, least of all now when we are confronted with all forms of cyber-bullying, not to mention the ever-increasing readiness to use weapons in conflict situations. Essentially, all that is required to be bullied is an abuse of power and intention to hurt. I am convinced that the escalating violence that we are witness to in society today, committed by both males and females, is due to the lax attitudes that educators have shown towards childhood bullying. To date, educators have tended not to step in early enough or to persist strongly enough to help aggressive children and teens to overcome their aggressive impulses.

The way forward as I see it is for the government to mandate schools to implement a whole school community approach to bullying and violence. We now know that such anti-bullying programmes work. By not investing in them we are behaving irresponsibly. If properly implemented they will prevent and significantly reduce the level of aggression, bullying and violence in not only our current school-going population, but in generations to come. If we commit to breaking the cycle of bullying and violence, we will most certainly be rewarded with a society where there is greater productivity and positive behaviour, less underachievement, psycho-somatic illness, depression, suicide, delinquency, domestic violence and societal violence. What can make more economic as well as ethical sense?

In order to achieve and sustain a successful nationwide implementation of a whole school community approach to bullying and violence, I believe our government's Department of Education and Skills would be wise to invest in a Centre of Excellence, which has the capacity to provide a resource for schools. The Centre, for example, can be given the responsibility to help schools to:

• develop and implement an effective anti-bullying policy, which attends to all forms of bullying;

- train a member of staff to become the school's anti-bullying co-ordinator;
- support and provide advice and guidance when problems arise that cannot be readily resolved.

Already in Ireland there are over sixty teachers who have had the necessary training to provide an effective resource to schools on a regional basis. Many of them contributed to the successful anti-bullying programme that was piloted in Donegal and to the IRCHSS-funded ABC nationwide programme. Others have gained a Masters in Education Degree in Aggression Studies from Trinity College Dublin. I am sure any or all of these professionals would be more than happy to act as a resource to schools around Ireland.

In this light, I hope the day will not be too far away when all of our school-going children and teenagers can benefit from a whole school community approach to bullying prevention. In the meantime, I hope this book has given you, as a reader, the determination and the confidence to tackle and prevent bullying behaviour among our youth.

APPENDIX

Bullying in Schools in Ireland: The Nationwide Study (1993–1994)

Percentage of pupils who have been bullied in school in each class/year during school term[1]

Level of Victimisation & Bullying											
Primary (N=9513)											
Class	Gender N			Pure Victim %			Pure Bully %			Bully-Victim %		
	Boys	Girls	Total	Boys	Girls	Total	Boys	Girls	Total	Boys	Girls	Total
3	324	349	673	20.7	24.4	22.6	12.7	5.7	9.1	23.8	14.6	19.0
4	1302	1311	2613	22.2	20.9	21.5	12.2	7.8	10.0	23.7	11.4	17.6
5	1607	1350	2957	18.4	16.1	17.3	15.5	8.0	11.8	19.8	8.7	14.3
6	1717	1548	3265	11.9	12.6	12.3	20.6	9.1	14.9	13.4	5.5	9.5
Total	4952	4561	9513	17.3	16.9	17.1	16.2	8.2	12.3	18.9	8.8	14.1

Post-primary (N=10538)											
Class	Gender N			Pure Victim %			Pure Bully %			Bully-Victim %		
	Boys	Girls	Total	Boys	Girls	Total	Boys	Girls	Total	Boys	Girls	Total
1	1986	2037	4023	17.2	10.0	13.5	12.7	4.9	8.8	6.0	1.5	3.7
2	1032	2012	3044	13.8	10.8	11.8	18.7	8.1	11.7	12.6	2.7	6.1
3	390	951	1341	12.3	10.2	10.8	23.6	8.7	13.0	7.9	1.7	3.5
4	172	502	674	7.0	8.6	8.2	20.3	8.6	11.6	9.9	.6	3.0
5	389	571	960	9.5	4.7	6.7	21.6	7.7	13.3	4.4	.9	2.3
6	99	397	496	8.1	7.1	7.3	21.2	5.5	8.7	6.1	1.5	2.4
Total	4068	6470	10538	14.5	9.5	11.4	16.7	7.0	10.7	7.9	1.8	4.1

Percentage of 'victims' in primary classes and post-primary years who report not having told their teacher or anyone at home about being bullied.

Primary Class	No of 'victims'	Have not told teachers	No of 'victims'	Have not told anyone at home
3	303	53.8	320	33.7
4	1075	62.0	1091	41.2
5	975	65.8	996	49.7
6	726	74.0	730	53.7

Post-primary Year	No of 'victims'	Have not told teachers	No of 'victims'	Have not told anyone at home
1	714	82.2	714	60.9
2	550	83.3	550	69.3
3	185	82.7	714	63.5
4	73	87.7	550	68.1
5	89	92.2	189	78.9
6	46	84.8	72	79.9

Note

1. For further details on the nationwide study, consult:
   - O'Moore, A.M., Kirkham, C. and Smith, M., 'Bullying Behaviour in Irish Schools: A Nationwide Study' in *Irish Journal of Psychology*, 18 (1997), pp. 141–169.
   - O'Moore, A.M., Kirkham, C. and Smith, M., 'Bullying in Schools in Ireland: A Nationwide Study, in *Irish Educational Studies*, 17 (1997), pp. 254–271.
   - O'Moore, M. and Kirkham, C., 'Self-Esteem and its Relationship to Bullying Behaviour' in *Aggressive Behaviour*, 27 (2001), pp. 269–283.

RECOMMENDED READING

Banks, S.R. and Thompson, C.L., *Educational Psychology For Teachers in Training*, New York: West Publishing Company, 1995.

Beane, A.L., *Bullying Prevention for Schools: A Step-by-Step Guide to Implementing a Successful Anti-Bullying Programme*, US: Jossey Bass, 2010.

Besag, V.E., *Understanding Girls' Friendships, Fights and Feuds: A Practical Approach to Girls' Bullying*, London: Open University Press, 2006.

Canter, L. and Canter, M., *Lee Canter's Assertive Discipline: Positive Behavior Management for Today's Classroom*, 3rd Edition, Los Angeles: Canter and Associates, 2001.

'Children and the Internet', *The Journal of Barnardos' Training and Resource Service*, Issue 1, 2008.

Cowie, H. and Jennifer, D., *Managing Violence in School: A Whole-School Approach to Best Practice*, London: Paul Chapman, 2007.

Cowie, H. and Wallace, P., *Peer Support in Action: From Bystanding to Standing By*, London: Sage Publications, 2000.

Department of Education and Science, *Guidelines on Countering Bullying Behaviour in Primary and Post-Primary Schools*, Dublin: The Stationery Office, 1993.

Department of Education and Science, *Guidelines on Violence in Schools: Circular Letter M18/99*, Dublin: Department of Education and Science, 1999.

Department of Education and Science, *School Matters, The Report of the Task Force on Student Behaviour in Second-Level Schools*, Dublin: Government Publications, 2006.

Dubin, N., *Asperger Syndrome and Bullying, Strategies and Solutions*, London: Jessica Kingsley Publishers, 2007.

228

Elliot, M. (ed.), *Bullying: A Practical Guide to Coping for Schools*, 3rd Edition, London: Pearson Education in Association with Kidscape, 2002.

Faupel, A., Herrick, E. and Sharp, P., *Anger Management: A Practical Guide*, London: David Fulton Publishers, 2000.

Fontana, D., *Psychology for Teachers*, 3rd Edition, London: Macmillan, 1995, in association with the British Psychological Society.

Fried, S. and Fried, P., *Bullies, Targets and Witnesses: Helping Children Break the Pain Chain*, New York: M. Evans and Company, Inc., 2003.

Gittins, C. (ed.), *Violence Reductions in Schools: How to Make a Difference*, Strasbourg: Council of Europe, 2006.

Goldstein, A.P., Glick, B., and Gibbs, J.C., *Aggression Replacement Training: A Comprehensive Intervention for Aggressive Youth*, Illinois: Research Press, 1998.

Heinrichs, R., *Perfect Targets: Asperger Syndrome and Bullying – Practical Solutions for Surviving the Social World*, Kansas: AutismAsperger Publishing Co., 2003.

Hoffman, L., *Empathy and Moral Development, Implications for Caring and Justice*, Cambridge: Cambridge University Press, 2007.

Hopkins, B., *Just Schools: A Whole School Approach to Restorative Justice*, London: Jessica Kingsley Publishers, 2004.

Humphreys, T., *Self-Esteem is Key to your Child's Education*, Cork: Tony Humphreys, 1993.

Kowalski, R.M., Limber, S.P. and Agatston, P.W., *Cyberbullying: Bullying in the Digital Age*, USA: Blackwell Publishing, 2008.

Lawrence, D., *Enhancing Self-Esteem in the Classroom*, London: Paul Chapman, 2006.

Levine, D.A., *Teaching Empathy: A Blueprint for Caring, Compassion, and Community*, US: Solution Tree Press, 2005.

Macklem, G.L., *Bullying and Teasing: Social Power in Children's Groups*, New York: Kluwer Academic/Plenum Publishers, 2004.

Maines, B. and Robinson, G., *Safe to Tell: Producing an Effective Anti-Bullying Policy in Schools*, Bristol: Lucky Duck Publishing, 2002.

McGuckin, C., and Lewis, C.A., 'Management of Bullying in Northern Ireland Schools: A Pre-legislative Survey' in *Educational Research*, 50 (2008), pp. 9–23.

McGuckin, C., O'Moore, M. and Crowley, N., *Cyber-Bullying: The Situation in Ireland*, Country Report, 2010 (http://www.cybertraining-project.org/page.php?lang=Enandpage=8).

229

McNamara, B.E. and McNamara, F.J., *Keys to Dealing with Bullies*, New York: Barrons, 1997.

National Educational Welfare Board, *Developing a Code of Behaviour: Guidelines for Schools*, Dublin: National Educational Welfare Board, 2008.

O'Moore, M., 'Critical Issues for Teacher Training to Counter Bullying and Victimisation in Ireland' in *Aggressive Behavior*, 26 (2000), pp. 99–111.

O'Moore, M. and Minton, S.J., *Dealing with Bullying in Schools: A Training Manual for Teachers, Parents and Other Professionals*, London: Paul Chapman, 2004.

O'Moore, M., *Report on the European Teachers' Seminar on 'Bullying in Schools'*, Strasbourg: Council for Cultural Co-operation, 1988.

Osterman, K. (ed.), *Indirect and Direct Aggression*, Frankfurt on Main: Peter Lang, 2010.

Pepler, D., and Craig, W., *Understanding and Addressing Bullying: An International Perspective*, Indiana: Author House, 2008.

Rogers, B., *Behaviour Management: A Whole School Approach*, London: Paul Chapman, 2004.

Shariff, S., *Cyber-Bullying: Issues and Solutions for the School, the Classroom and the Home*, New York: Routledge, 2008.

Sharry, J., *Positive Parenting: Bringing Up Responsible Well-Behaved and Happy Children*, Dublin: Veritas, 1999.

Smith, P.K., Pepler, D. and Rigby, K., *Bullying in Schools: How Effective Can Interventions Be?*, Cambridge: Cambridge University Press, 2004.

Stallard, P., *Anxiety: Cognitive Behaviour Therapy with Children and Young People*, London: Routledge, 2009.

Sullivan, K., *The Anti-Bullying Handbook*, 2nd Edition, London: Sage Publications, 2010.

The Irish Association of Suicidology, *Suicide Prevention in Schools: Best Practice Guidelines*, 2000.

World Health Organisation, 'Young People's Health in Context: Health Behaviour in School-aged Children (HBSC) Study, Intermediate Report from 2001/2002 Survey' in *Health Policy for Children and Adolescents*, 4 (2004).

Books that can be read by a young person alone or together with an adult:
Auer, J., *Standing Up to Peer Pressure*, Indiana: Abbey Press, 2003.

Jackson, J.S., *Bye-Bye, Bully: A Kid's Guide for Dealing with Bullies*, Indiana: Abbey Press, 2003.

McAuslan, F. and Nicholson, P., *The Resolving Bullying Book*, Dublin: Veritas, 2010.

McAuslan, F. and Nicholson, P., *The Resolving Anger Book*, Dublin: Veritas, 2010.

O'Moore, M . and Minton, S.J., 'What all Young People Need to Know', Chapter 5 in *Dealing with Bullying in Schools: A Training Manual for Teachers, Parents and Other Professionals*, London: Paul Chapman, 2004.

O'Neal, J., *Respect, Dare to Care, Share, and Be Fair!*, Indiana: Abbey Press, 2001.

Sanders, P., *Dealing With Bullying*, London: Aladdin/Watts, 2004.

Stones, R., *Don't Pick on Me*, London: Piccadilly Press, 1993.

Online Resources

Anti-Bullying Campaign: Tools for Teachers: www.antibullyingcampaign.ie.

Helen Cowie, Ozhan Oztug and Mike O'Driscoll, *Managing School Violence and Bullying: A Whole School Approach for Teachers:* www.vistop.org/ebook.

Conor McGuckin, Mona O'Moore and Niall Crowley, *Cyberbullying: The Situation in Ireland*: www.cybertraining-project.org.

Mona O'Moore, and Stephen James Minton, *Elements of a Whole School Approach: Working with Parents*: www.vistop.org/ebook.

VISTA, Violence in Schools Training Action: www.vista.org.

Audio-Visual Resources

DVDs:

Bully For You, Triplevision Production Ltd., for BBC Northern Ireland.

Bullying in Schools: Six Methods of Intervention, Loggerhead Films (www.loggerheadfilms.co.uk), Ken Rigby.

Silent Witnesses, a DVD and workbook to assist schools and parents in preventing bullying. Produced by Animo Communications in association with the Anti-Bullying Centre, Trinity College Dublin.

CDs:

The Diary of Leanne Wolfe, RTÉ Radio 1 – Documentary on One, 2008: www.rte.ie/doconone.

Useful Websites for Advice and Guidance

www.anti-bullyingalliance.org

http://www.antibullying.net/cyberbullying1.htm

www.internetsafety.ie

www.abc.tcd.ie

www.barnardos.ie

www.bpl.org/kids/Netiquette.htm

www.bullying.co.uk

www.childline.ie

www.cybertraining-project.org

www.mykidstime.ie

www.niabf.org.uk

www.parentline.ie

www.respectme.org

www.kidscape.org.uk

www.teachernet.gov.uk/publications

www.antibullyingcampaign.ie

www.resolvingbooks.com

Agencies for Seeking Help

Anti-Bullying Centre: www.abc.tcd.ie.

www.counsellingdirectory.com

Childline

Parentline

www.reachout.com